THE MORTAL WORM

Kennikat Press
National University Publications
Literary Criticism Series

General Editor

John E. Becker
Fairleigh Dickinson University

Elias Schwartz

THE MORTAL WORM
Shakespeare's Master Theme

National University Publications
KENNIKAT PRESS // 1977
Port Washington, N. Y. // London

FOR MARTHA, PETER, PAUL, DAVID, AND DANNY

Manufactured in the United States of America

Published by
Kennikat Press Corp.
Port Washington, N. Y./London

Library of Congress Cataloging in Publication Data

Schwartz, Elias, 1923–
   The mortal worm.

   (Kennikat Press national university publications)
(Literary criticism series)
   Bibliography: p.
   Includes index.
   1. Shakespeare, William, 1564–1616–Criticism and
interpretation. I. Title.
PR2976.S324   822.3'3   76-40423
ISBN 0-8046-9137-1

CONTENTS

FOREWORD

I focus in this book on a cluster of basic Shakespearean themes, as they are expressed in a series of plays written between 1599 and 1611. These themes continually recur in Shakespeare's work, interacting in complex and changing ways. They constitute, in my view, a nucleus of emotional and artistic energy which gives distinctive form to all of Shakespeare's work. The plays of the period 1599-1611 (as G. Wilson Knight observes in *The Sovereign Flower*) form a sequence in which "groups of plays and single plays shed mutual light on each other. The sequence is impressive and compelling, and evidences clearly some purpose in the creating power which we name 'Shakespeare'."

I start with the Sonnets because there the seeds of most later developments are surprisingly present. I then consider a series of six plays: *Julius Caesar, Troilus and Cressida, Othello, King Lear, Antony and Cleopatra,* and *The Winter's Tale*. The danger in the sort of study I propose is that I may be led to fit unique works into an a priori thematic pattern. I can only plead that I have tried not to confuse my own attitudes with those of Shakespeare—those present, I mean, in his work. Throughout I attempt to infer rather than to impose, and to infer by way of structural analysis of particular works.

I do start with the belief that throughout his work, and especially in the works I take up, Shakespeare was concerned with the basic question, "What is the meaning of human life?" This concern takes its particular Shakespearean form in connection with a number of recurrent thematic oppositions: time and eternity, love and death, honor and power, mortality and immortality. The nature of these oppositions will become clearer, I hope, in the course of this study. I should say now that each of these pairs refers to an area of value, rather than to a particular idea or feeling. *Love*, for example, as I shall be using the term, does not refer only to passionate relations between human beings. It refers to the whole emotional and intuitive side of human experience—usually opposed, in Shakespeare, to the rational, egoistic, aggressive side. Each of the other terms also stands for an emotionally freighted cluster of attitudes, rather than for any precisely definable idea.

In this general approach to Shakespeare, as will already be apparent, I am following the pioneer work of G. Wilson Knight. Yet I have serious reservations about Knight's criticism; he tends (I think) to move too quickly into the realm of transcendent meaning, not adequately grounding such leaps in structural analysis. I therefore differ with many of Knight's interpretations, even though I applaud his main intention to uncover the innermost meaning of Shakespeare's work.

Four of the chapters and Appendix B have been published, in slightly different form, as follows: chapters 2 and 7 appeared in *College English* in the issues of January, 1958 and April, 1962. Chapter 3 was published in *Studies in Philology* for July, 1972. Chapter 4 was published in *Studies in English Literature* for Spring, 1970. Appendix B appeared in *English Language Notes* for September, 1969. I am grateful to the editors of these journals for permission to use this material. Throughout I have used Kittredge's 1936 text, changing only his non-syllabic *'d* to *ed*.

I should like to record my thanks to my colleague Francis X. Newman for valuable advice and criticism, and to my wife Marjory for her help in editing the manuscript.

THE MORTAL WORM

Hast thou the pretty worm of Nilus there
That kills and pains not?

Truly, I have him. But I would not be the party that should desire you to touch him, for his biting is immortal. Those that do die of it do seldom or never recover.

Antony and Cleopatra V.ii.243-48

CHAPTER ONE

SEEDS

I want to begin by examining four groups of sonnets, three from the Fair Youth series, one from the Dark Woman series. My selection of these is not entirely arbitrary: they embody in more or less explicit form the themes or thematic oppositions with which this book as a whole is concerned. I am going to ignore the many sonnets which do not directly bear on these themes. And I am putting aside altogether the questions of conventionality and topicality. Just as we may regard the plays as works of art having objective, public meanings quite independent of any personal or topical allusion, so the Sonnets, too, may be supposed to have a meaning coextensive with their formal structure. The "only begetter" and the mortal moon, then, will not concern us. We are interested only in the meaning of these poems as poems.

The three groups from the Fair Youth series are all about love and death. They vary a good deal in quality and in "seriousness." But whatever their individual quality, they seem to stand apart from the rest by reason both of their thematic similarity and their cumulative power. (One result of this power is that one gets the impression that there are more sonnets of this type than there actually are.) They are all ostensibly love poems, yet they are most of them encumbered with a profound sadness, a sadness almost always connected with the poet's sense of time's inexorable triumph over beauty and life. The true theme of these sonnets is Time the Destroyer. Against Time (and his ally Death) the poet invokes three kinds of defense: "breed," the eternizing power of poetry, and the staying power of true love.[1]

The sonnets in the breed group seem the most conventional, the least distinguished as verse. Yet even here there are moments of heightened feeling, usually connected with the sense of time's depredation. Sonnet 12, for example, breaks out of its low-keyed context in the third quatrain:

> Then of thy beauty do I question make
> That thou among the wastes of time must go,
> Since sweets and beauties do themselves forsake
> And die as fast as they see others grow,
>> And nothing 'gainst Time's scythe can make defence
>> Save breed, to brave him when he takes thee hence.

The dying which is universal in nature becomes, in line 10, a home truth: the poet realizes that the wastes of time include the beloved. Notice that the couplet does not assert the triumph of breed over time—breed only "braves" time. And notice also that the strongest feeling in the poem coincides with the poet's recognition of time's power.

In the other sonnets of this group, there is more emphasis on the beloved's duty—a kind of moral obligation—to preserve his beauty in despite of time. But what recurs insistently and with consistent eloquence is the poet's obsession with time, with the universal mortality of nature:

> When forty winters shall besiege thy brow
> And dig deep trenches in thy beauty's field,
> Thy youth's proud livery, so gazed on now,
> Will be a tattered weed, of small worth held ... (2)

> Look in thy glass, and tell the face thou viewest
> Now is the time that face should form another ... (3)

> For never-resting time leads summer on
> To hideous winter and confounds him there,
> Sap checked with frost and lusty leaves quite gone,
> Beauty o'ersnowed and bareness everywhere ... (5)

> Then let not winter's ragged hand deface
> In thee thy summer ere thou be distilled ... (6)

Among the eternizing sonnets, too, the moments of strongest feeling are connected with time's encroachment on life. In the sestet of 15, it is precisely the poet's sense of mortality that makes the beloved seem precious to him:

> Then the conceit of this inconstant stay
> Sets you most rich in youth before my sight,
> Where wasteful Time debateth with Decay
> To change your day of youth to sullied night.
> And all in war with Time for love of you,
> As he takes from you, I ingraft you new.

After the rather eloquent account of time's ravages, the couplet here seems anticlimactic, almost an afterthought.

In 19 we get a series of imperatives, ordering time to do what he will do in any event: "Devouring Time, blunt thou the lion's paws. . . ." The poet, it turns out, is making a kind of bargain with time: time may destroy all other creatures if he will only save the beloved. Then, in the couplet, a "witty" reversal:

> Yet do thy worst, old Time. Despite thy wrong,
> My love shall in my verse ever live young.

The claim does not carry much conviction—especially after the grandiloquence of the earlier lines. What sticks in the mind is the powerful evocation of time's power.

In 55 the eternizing idea seems much more convincing, partly because it comes much earlier in the sonnet's development. Here there is a concurrent contempt for time and exultation in the poet's own sense of creative power:

> Not marble, nor the gilded monuments
> Of princes, shall outlive this powerful rhyme;
> But you shall shine more bright in these contents
> Than unswept stone, besmeared with sluttish time.

But 55 is unusual in its purity, its sharp focus on the old Horatian theme. A more realistic and more typically Shakespearean handling of it appears in 63, where the poet stoically faces the fact that time will one day destroy the beloved. Time's victory will be qualified only by the immortality conferred by memory (that is, by poetry):

> Against my love shall be as I am now,
> With Time's injurious hand crushed and o'erworn;
> When hours have drained his blood and filled his brow
> With lines and wrinkles; when his youthful morn
> Hath travelled on to age's steepy night,
> And all those beauties whereof now he's king

Are vanishing, or vanished out of sight,
Stealing away the treasure of his spring—
For such a time do I now fortify
Against confounding age's cruel knife,
That he shall never cut from memory
My sweet love's beauty, though my lover's life.
His beauty shall in these black lines be seen,
And they shall live, and he in them still green.

In 60 we get even greater emphasis on the certainty of the beloved's dissolution: it is only after twelve lines of sad and eloquent contemplation of images of mutability and decay that the couplet slightly mitigates the sense of mortality:

And yet to times in hope my verse shall stand,
Praising thy worth, despite his cruel hand.

There is a curious illogicality in 18 which has been obscured, I think, by the sonnet's extraordinary sweetness of phrase and lovely rhythms. In the octave the beloved is said to be more lovely than other fair things, which implies that the beloved is part of nature and so shares their common fate. Yet in the sestet, the beloved is set apart from the others, not because of the beloved's special merit, but because of the *poet's*. The object of praise, in short, changes from the beloved to the poet's art. Here is the sonnet.

Shall I compare thee to a summer's day?
Thou art more lovely and more temperate.
Rough winds do shake the darling buds of May,
And summer's lease hath all too short a date.
Sometime too hot the eye of heaven shines,
And often is his gold complexion dimmed;
And every fair from fair sometime declines,
By chance or nature's changing course untrimmed;
But thy eternal summer shall not fade
Nor lose possession of that fair thou owest,
Nor shall Death brag thou wand'rest in his shade
When in eternal lines to time thou growest.
So long as men can breathe or eyes can see,
So long lives this, and this gives life to thee.

How shall we justify the shift from the loved one's merely natural superiority to the assertion of transcendence or immortality? And how justify the shift from praise of the beloved to praise of the poet's art? How seriously, finally, are we to take the poet's claim to eternizing power?

As to the last question, we ought to notice that the usual sadness is absent from this sonnet, that we get here rather an exultant joy, apparently related to the poet's intimation of immortality. This seems somewhat different from the "professional" exultation of the Horatian 55. It is as though the poet exults not so much in his art as in the beloved, not so much in his power as in his intuition that love puts him in touch with eternity.

This intuition is mystical—it cannot be logically explained. And that may be why the sonnet combines an elliptical thought pattern with powerful feeling. Yet there is a kind of patent logic: the beloved evokes the poet's love, which is the "cause," the enabling force, of the poet's art. The beloved is therefore the ultimate cause of the poet's eternizing power and of his own immortality. The poet's love is (literally) *ex-pressed* in his verse, and the beloved is (essentially) embodied in it. So it is right for the poet to shift from praise of the beloved to praise of his own art. For the poet's art is virtually a passive instrument in the attainment of immortality. The active force is the beloved's beauty—both through its evocation of love and through its immanence in the verse.[2]

In most of these ways 107 is similar to 18. Yvor Winters thinks line 11 ("Since, spite of him, I'll live in this poor rhyme") is a nonsequitur: "There is not the remotest connection between Southampton's release from prison . . . and Shakespeare's making himself and Southampton immortal in verse."[3] But this incoherence is only apparent, especially if we look at 107 in the light of what we discovered about 18. At the start the poet proclaims, in a tone of serene confidence, that his love has survived despite his own fears and the world's anticipation of its demise. In the second quatrain he gives examples of the dire predictions that have, in the event, proven wrong. Then in line 10 the apparent nonsequitur: "My love looks fresh, and Death to me subscribes. . . ." The survival of the poet's love (his affection for his beloved, not for Southampton, as Winters has it) is of course not equivalent to his defeating death. But here, again, the deep exultancy points to the latent (and true) meaning: love's "truth" is proved by its enduring, and it is also the creative source of the eternizing poetry in and through which he attains immortality.[4]

Further light is thrown on this process by those sonnets which speak of the poet's distilling the beloved's "truth" in his verse, as the essence of a flower is distilled in its perfume. The "truth" thus distilled is preserved forever and is in a sense finer than the actual flower and person—a kind of Platonic Idea. Sonnet 54 is a good example:

O, how much more doth beauty beauteous seem
By that sweet ornament which truth doth give!
The rose looks fair, but fairer we it deem
For that sweet odour which doth in it live.
The canker blooms have full as deep a dye
As the perfumed tincture of the roses,
Hang on such thorns, and play as wantonly
When summer's breath their masked buds discloses;
But, for their virtue only is their show,
They live unwooed and unrespected fade,
Die to themselves. Sweet roses do not so:
Of their sweet deaths are sweetest odours made.
    And so of you, beauteous and lovely youth,
    When that shall fade, my verse distills your truth.

The essence of the rose (its truth) is created out of its death. The beautiful thing is thus made eternal, its real being distilled. In the poet's case this comes about partly as a result of the beloved's truth (*truth* seems to mean both essence and constancy, an important association for the constancy sonnets). His constancy is in a sense the essence of his beauty; it is the inmost, perduring reality and is opposed, here and elsewhere in Shakespeare, to outward "show"—falsehood, illusion, unreality. So, in Sonnet 5, "flowers distilled, though they with winter meet,/Leese but their show—their substance still lives sweet."[5]   In 18 and other eternizing sonnets the means of distillation is the poet's art. But this art depends for its effectiveness on the poet's love, and, ultimately, on the constancy or truth of the beloved. To the old idea of art's conferring immortality, Shakespeare adds the idea of love's necessary presence as creative cause. Here, as later in "The Phoenix and Turtle," love and constancy are intimately related to each other and to the eternizing power of poetry.

In the sonnets which celebrate the constancy of the poet's love, but in which the eternizing power of poetry is not invoked (our third group), there is no claim to immortality whatever. True love, the poet says, does not change as all other things change; but it is not, alas, immune to death. Sonnet 116, the most famous of this group, begins with a magnificent description of true love:

Let me not to the marriage of true minds
Admit impediments. Love is not love
Which alters when it alteration finds
Or bends with the remover to remove.
O, no! it is an ever-fixed mark

That looks on tempests and is never shaken;
It is the star to every wand'ring bark,
Whose worth's unknown, although his height be taken.

But then, in the sestet, though the poet asserts that "Love's not Time's fool," he nevertheless recognizes that beauty and life itself are subject to time. And love bears it out—but only to the edge of doom. Beauty dies, lovers die, and love (presumably) dies with the lover. That is why (we surmise) truth and beauty can be eternized only in poetry.[6]

Sonnet 124, another of the constancy sonnets, contains the most explicit statement of any on the opposition between love and power. Since this is one of the most persistent themes in Shakespeare's tragedies, the sonnet deserves careful study here.

If my dear love were but the child of state,
It might for Fortune's bastard be unfathered,
As subject to Time's love or to Time's hate,
Weeds among weeds, or flowers with flowers gathered.
No, it was builded far from accident;
It suffers not in smiling pomp, nor falls
Under the blow of thralled discontent,
Whereto the inviting time our fashion calls.
It fears not policy, that heretic
Which works on leases of short-numbered hours,
But all alone stands hugely politic,
That it nor grows with heat nor drowns with showers.
   To this I witness call the fools of time,
   Which die for goodness, who have lived for crime.

Two vexing cruxes in the sonnet need not concern us.[7] The general meaning is clear enough. The poet asserts that his love, unlike all the children of "state," is not subject to time and fortune. The children of state are subject to change (in one sense of "state") or dependent on political favor (in another). No claim is made to immortality, but, as in 116, love is clearly superior to all else and, as always, its superiority lies in its resistance to mutability. Love is not the fool of time, is, in some sense, outside the realm of time. And so it stands "hugely politic" in contrast with those who are time's subjects, fools, slaves. This exemption of love from time's power (for the time of life, at any rate) is of some importance, for, as we shall see, it is the counter-idea to the idea of lust as time-binding. We ought to notice also the tone of deep certitude in the poet's assertion of the hugely politic wisdom of choosing love as against any worldy good.

The concluding sonnet of the Fair Youth series (126) is not a member of any of our groups, but it is perhaps the most explicit avowal of man's utter defenselessness against time. Its unique stanzaic structure (twelve lines rimed in couplets) and its thematic finality make it a fitting conclusion to the Fair Youth series. The poet recognizes as illusion the idea that the beloved can ultimately defeat time. Nature—though she be "sovereign mistress over wrack"—is still time's subject and must inevitably render up the beloved.

> O thou my lovely boy, who in thy power
> Dost hold Time's fickle glass, his sickle hour;
> Who has by waning grown, and therein show'st
> Thy lovers withering as thy sweet self grow'st,
> If Nature (sovereign mistress over wrack),
> As thou goest onwards, still will pluck thee back,
> She keeps thee to this purpose, that her skill
> May time disgrace, and wretched minutes kill.
> Yet fear her, O thou minion of her pleasure!
> She may detain, but not still keep, her treasure;
> Her audit, though delayed, answered must be,
> And her quietus is to render thee.

The three thematic groups I have described were probably not intended as groups. But for our purposes that does not matter. We may still fairly infer from these sonnets—from their special eloquence and their intimate thematic relations—that one of Shakespeare's earliest dominant themes (and obsessions?) is the inexorable power of time. That is what gives the Sonnets as a whole their distinctive and poignant sadness. That is what lies behind the most memorable and most beautiful sonnets of the Fair Youth series. Wallace Stevens's phrase—"Death is the mother of beauty"—thus applies to the Sonnets in a sense different from that intended in "Sunday Morning." The obsession with death is the creative idea, the motivating intuition, of the Sonnets.

Of the poet's three "defenses" against death, the defense by way of procreation seems the most formulary, the least deeply felt. The defense through true love—through constancy—is presented with great emotional power, but it provides only temporary respite. It enables the poet to brave, but not to defeat, time. The defense by way of art, through the eternizing power of poetry, involves something mysterious, an intimation of meanings deeper and more complex than those to be found in Horace. The immortality promised by our ever-living poet has something to do with Plato, or with neo-Platonism. (I leave the question to those more expert than I.) The beloved in these sonnets is both a creative source for, and a presence in, the poet's verse, a *real* cause and a *real* presence. That is precisely why the poet connects his love with immortality. Like all lovers, the poet intuits that his love lifts him outside of time, puts him in touch with eternity. He expresses his love and embodies his beloved in his poetry. And *in* his poetry—so claims the poet—the beloved will live forever. Very strange. Very mystical. Yet these ideas seem quite seriously intended in a number of the sonnets. And they will reappear in Shakespeare's work at the very end of his career.

The sonnets in the Dark Woman series which bitterly recount the poet's passion and enslavement to lust are in most ways the obverse of the constancy sonnets. The woman is notoriously faithless, not fair, not worthy of love. Yet the poet cannot control his passion: his lust overcomes his hatred and revulsion. And his lust subjects him to time, distorts his perceptions, leads him into the realm of lies, of illusion. Sonnet 129, which might serve well as a general introduction to the series, is structured in terms of the temporal aspects of lust:

> Th'expense of spirit in a waste of shame
> Is lust in action; and till action, lust
> Is perjured, murd'rous, bloody, full of blame,
> Savage, extreme, rude, cruel, not to trust;
> Enjoyed no sooner but despised straight;
> Past reason hunted, and no sooner had,
> Past reason hated, as a swallowed bait,
> On purpose laid to make the taker mad;
> Mad in pursuit, and in possession so;
> Had, having, and in quest to have, extreme;
> A bliss in proof—and proved, a very woe;
> Before, a joy proposed; behind, a dream.
>> All this the world well knows; yet none knows well
>> To shun the Heaven that leads men to this Hell.

Lust imposes an enslavement to time because, unlike love, it belongs to the realm of mortality, the realm of change and decay. So the poet's revulsion is not merely sexual disgust; it is, in a way, a resistance to time and to death.

It is also a revulsion at illusion and lies. Again and again the poet bitterly notes the delusion under which he labors, the lies lovers tell and live.

> If thy soul check thee that I come so near,
> Swear to thy blind soul that I was thy Will,
> And will, thy soul knows, is admitted there. (136)

> When my love swears that she is made of truth
> I do believe her, though I know she lies . . . (138)

> Bear thine eyes straight, though thy proud heart go wide. (140)

> My love is as a fever, longing still
> For that which longer nurseth the disease . . . (147)

> O me, what eyes hath Love put in my head,
> Which have no correspondence with true sight! (148)

> O, from what power hast thou this powerful might
> With insufficiency my heart to sway? (150)

The bitterness of these sonnets is utterly different from Petrarchan lament. This is revulsion, not frustrated passion; the lover does not long for sweet delusion, but defines and judges his passion to be delusion. Unlike the troubador, the lover of the bitter sonnets takes no joy in his pain, does not acquiesce in his frustration. And the ideal by which this passion is judged is not the dark, death-directed passion of Tristan; it is rather the true love of the constancy sonnets, which, remember, is not time's fool. Perhaps it is not fanciful to suppose that 146, the only sonnet in the whole sequence which might be called religious, is a sort of envoi to the Dark Woman series. For in this sonnet the poet calls upon his soul to give up the goods of the body—which will die—and attend to its own good.

> So shalt thou feed on Death, that feeds on men,
> And Death once dead, there's no more dying then.

What should be noted, finally, about love in the Sonnets, is the astounding constrast between the *feeling* in the Fair Youth series and in the Dark Woman series. In the former there is a remarkable absence of passion, of sexual feeling; there is simply a rejoicing in the beloved's existence. The poet wants nothing, asks for nothing, almost loses his own selfhood.

> Being your slave, what should I do but tend
> Upon the hours and times of your desire?
> I have no precious time at all to spend,
> Nor services to do, till you require. (57)

The most powerful sonnets of the second series, on the other hand, express and define an engrossing sexual passion which the poet knows degrades and humiliates him but which he is unable to resist. The general impession here is one of intense sexual revulsion. As a consequence, the Sonnets as a whole convey the impression of a radical separation of the flesh and spirit, a separation and opposition between true love and lust. In the following chapters we shall note some surprising changes in Shakespeare's handling of this relationship.

CHAPTER TWO

JULIUS CAESAR

Julius Caesar was written around 1599, toward the close of the period (1590-98) during which most of the Sonnets were written, and just after *Henry V*, the last of the Lancastrian history plays. It is the first of a series of great tragedies. In the plays that precede *Caesar*, the themes that run through the Sonnets have a kind of shadowy presence. In the histories they are subdued to the larger aim of celebrating Elizabeth's reign and the providential event leading up to it. Yet their presence is palpable in Shakespeare's persistent ambivalence toward the chief figures of the histories: the two Richards, Bolingbroke, Hotspur, Falstaff, and Hal.

Richard II has an emphatic political focus; but beneath the surface we may discern an intense interest in the personal world of human feeling and human personality. This double interest is reflected in the play's formal split into two generically divergent parts. The first two acts are formally the beginning of a history play: Richard is a bad king simply, Bolingbroke is a wronged nobleman fighting for the right. But when Richard's fall is imminent (at III.ii), the nature of the play changes. Richard suddenly becomes a sympathetic human being as well as a king:

> I weep for joy
> To stand upon my kingdom once again.
> Dear earth, I do salute thee ... (III.ii.4-6)

Richard has just returned from Ireland to find rebellion at home. He has never shown any love before for England, nor has he seemed capable of love for any object but himself. Yet now he is a loving protector of English earth, God's anointed king. This is not hypocrisy: he is simply a different

14

character, and the play has changed its nature. Now Bolingbroke is no longer a wronged nobleman; he is a calculating, efficient, cold-blooded politician.

At the end of the play, through self-knowledge and humility, Richard attains true tragic status; he sums up:

> Whate'er I be,
> Nor I, nor any man that but man is,
> With nothing shall be pleased till he be eased
> With being nothing. (V.v.38-41)

Richard thus achieves a kind of moral victory at his death, whereas our final view of Bolingbroke makes us wonder whether his victory is worth much. Bolingbroke's revulsion at Richard's murder is unfeigned. The murderer tells him: "From your own mouth did I this deed." And the king replies: "They love not poison that do poison need. . . ." In Bolingbroke, and even in his son (who is in every way the "ideal" king), we may discern that dehumanization which seems, in Shakespeare, to be inseparable from the pursuit and possession of political power. That is a theme which pervades the tragedies.

I do not mean to say that there is any simple opposition in Shakespeare between the personal and the political, between love and honor, between the private and the public goals of men. There is, rather, in the work of this period a multiplicity of values and a constant ambivalence toward them. True love is, of course, always opposed to lust and is always one of the greatest goods. But it is not always opposed to the flesh, as it is in the Sonnets. Love sometimes includes the body—as it does, for example, in *Romeo and Juliet*. And the pursuit of power is not always opposed to personal values simply. In Hotspur (as, later, in Coriolanus) it is transformed into the pursuit of honor—though the question of the "truth" of honor in such figures remains, I suspect, equivocal.

Ambiguity and ambivalence are evident throughout the Lancastrian histories—in the contrast between Hotspur and Hal and in the subtler contrasts between Falstaff and them both. Though Hotspur is a traitor, he is yet, aesthetically, a more attractive person than Hal. And though we recognize the value of Hal's kingly qualities, we also see the ways in which his humanity has been subordinated to his political function. That is one reason why Hotspur's single-minded pursuit of honor seems, by contrast, to stem from a kind of personal purity, a devotion analogous to that of the true lover. So, too, there is an underlying truth of perception in the popular reaction to Hal's rejection of Falstaff. Hal *must* reject Falstaff and all he represents—we recognize and accept that. And we recognize too the viciousness of the fat man's vices. But at the same time Falstaff's warmth and vitality, his commonsense views of war and the pursuit of pleasure, serve to undermine the passion of Hotspur as well as the cold, politic virtues of Hal. "There's honor for you!" says Falstaff, pointing to the corpse of Sir Walter Blunt. "Give me life," he says, and his voice is as persuasive as anyone's.[1]

In *Julius Caesar*, for the first time since the Sonnets, the counter-poised values of love and honor, the demands of public good and private need, are presented in more or less "pure" form, unobscured by the celebrative aims of the history plays. For the play is a tragedy, aiming at its own formal perfection and coming near to its achievement. A kind of ambivalence persists here, not, as before, toward the values represented in the play, but toward the first of a long line of tragic heroes.

That Caesar is not the protagonist of the play may, I think, be taken as settled. But Caesar's character—whether we are supposed to see him as the noblest man in the world or as a thrasonical braggart or as something in between—this has not been settled; and on this depend our view of Brutus, our view of the morality of, and motive for, the murder, and, ultimately, our interpretation of the play. There are two causes of Caesar's problematic status. One is our egalitarian and democratic bias, which Shakespeare did not share, but which, in viewing a play such as this, we find difficult to suppress. Our "natural" tendency is to sympathize with those who would put down tyranny; but Shakespeare's sympathies, so far as we can judge from his work as a whole, were different. He believed, like most of his fellows, in monarchy and in hierarchy, and though purely political questions do not figure importantly in our play, yet political attitudes affect our vision of the action and of the characters, as they affected Shakespeare's.

The other cause, an intrinsic rather than an extrinsic one, is the ambiguity resulting from Shakespeare's technique of characterizing Caesar, his apparent "regression" to a more "primitive" method than that which, at this point in his career, he generally uses. I refer to the apparent egotism implied in Caesar's self-descriptions:

> Would he were fatter! But I fear him not.
> Yet if my name were liable to fear,
> I do not know the man I should avoid
> So soon as that spare Cassius. (I.ii.198-201)

> I rather tell thee what is to be feared
> Than what I fear; for always I am Ceasar. (I.ii.211-12)

> Danger knows full well
> That Caesar is more dangerous than he.
> We are two lions littered in one day . . . (II.ii.44f.)

> These couchings and these lowly courtesies
> Might fire the blood of ordinary men . . . (III.i.36f.)

> I could be well moved if I were as you;   ·
> If I could pray to move, prayers would move me;
> But I am constant as the Northern Star . . . (III.i.58f.)

These speeches have a kind of crudity.[2] If they are direct, self-characterizing speeches of the sort Schücking defined, they are palpably less adroit
than others in the same play. I am thinking of Brutus'

> If it be aught toward the general good,
> Set honour in one eye and death i'th'other,
> And I will look on both indifferently;
> For let the gods so speed me as I love
> The name of honour more than I fear death. (I.ii.85-89)

The difference is not easy to describe. In Caesar's speeches the sentiments
seem *detached* from the speaker—as though another person were describ-
ing him. Brutus' speech, though it accurately describes the speaker, seems
to stem from the character it describes. It is, in short, both directly and
indirectly characterizing. We are not brought up short, as in Caesar's
speeches, by a sense of incongruity—between Caesar's eminence and
dignity and the "crudity" of his self-description.

    I think we must take this apparent ineptness in the characterization of
Caesar as a survival of an earlier and simpler mode of dramatic exposition,
and that we must, therefore, take his self-characterization at face value.
(I shall suggest below a possible reason for this "regression.") A number of
features of the play tend to support this view. First of all, Shakespeare
generally shows Caesar to be more, rather than less, noble than Plutarch's
figure.[3] Furthermore, no one in the play calls Caesar an egotist or braggart. The only charge levelled against him, by friend or foe, is that he is
ambitious. The "objective" Artemidorus remarks (II.iii.13-14): "My heart
laments that virtue cannot live/Out of the teeth of emulation." And Brutus finds no fault with Caesar the man. He would not have him become
king, he tells Cassius, "yet I love him well." For Brutus, it is not Caesar's
character, but the possibility of political change that threatens the Republic:

> for my part
> I know no personal cause to spurn at him . . .

> And to speak truth of Caesar,
> I have not known when his affections swayed
> More than his reason. (II.i.10-11,19-21)

Even Cassius imputes no fault of *character* to Caesar. His "levelling" political views are a (rather ineffective) disguise for his envy and hatred, his sense of not having achieved the eminence of Caesar. There is a transparent irony in his

> but for my single self,
> I had as lief not be as live to be
> In awe of such a thing as I myself. (I.ii.94-96)

Cassius thus betrays his poor estimate of himself, to which level he would reduce all men—especially those, like Caesar, who clearly surpass him in worth. Cassius goes on to point out Caesar's *physical* deficiencies, an "argument" which enhances our sense of Caesar as a man of extraordinary will and personal achievement. Indeed, Shakespeare's emphasis throughout the play on Caesar's infirmities of body serves as an index of his superiority to handicaps.

The most cogent piece of "evidence" for this view of Caesar is Cassius' more or less direct speech at the end of I.ii. It is similar in function, structure, and placement to Iago's direct soliloquies in the first two acts of *Othello*.

> Well, Brutus, thou art noble; yet I see
> Thy honourable mettle may be wrought
> From that it is disposed. Therefore it is meet
> That noble minds keep ever with their likes;
> For who so firm that cannot be seduced?
> Caesar doth bear me hard; but he loves Brutus.
> If I were Brutus now and he were Cassius,
> He should not humour me. I will this night . . . (I,ii,312-19)

The speech establishes unequivocally Cassius' villain status and Brutus' "seduction" into the conspiracy. It establishes also the dishonorable motives of the conspirators (excepting Brutus), and so confirms our view of Caesar as the foremost man of all the world, analogous to an Elizabethan monarch (a good one).[4]

One other possibility must be considered. Apart from the "ennobling" effect of Caesar's all-too-human weaknesses, they may work in another way. I am thinking of Caesar's inconsistency and his giving in to Decius' flattery (II.ii) in going to the Senate. This in itself is hardly ennobling. But it points, I think, the distinction between Caesar the political figure ("Caesar's spirit") and the ordinary man who has assumed that role. All men, whatever their political status, are merely men, subject to the same limitations and needs as other men. But those who have attained the status of Caesar have also a suprapersonal being. They gather into themselves the wills and the desires—the well-being—of all the members of the state. This is the cursed spite that Hamlet refers to, which makes it incumbent upon him to set things right.[5] I suggest that one aim of the equivocal self-characterizing speeches (where Caesar often refers to himself in the third person) is to reveal this, for Shakespeare, real distinction. It is also worth noting that, though the play is "framed" by a political situation, its primary focus and import is personal. And this import, the conflict between political idealism and personal commitment, is fought out and resolved in the play's protagonist.[6]

In his perceptive (and somewhat cloudy) study of the play, G. Wilson Knight observes that *Julius Caesar*

is charged highly with a general eroticism. All the people are "lovers." This love is emotional, fiery, but not exactly sexual, not physically passionate: even Portia and Brutus love with a gentle companionship rather than with any passion . . . the human element is often one of gentle sentiment, melting hearts, tears, and the soft fire of love. . . . The word "lover" is amazingly frequent, sometimes meaning little more than "friend," but always helping to build a general atmosphere of comradeship and affection.[7]

To those acquainted with traditional views of the play, this must seem, at the least, astonishing. But I think Knight is on to something: the feature of the play which he here discriminates is a key to its meaning, to its central focus on the conflict of head and heart, on the opposition between the personal world of feeling and the impersonal world of ideals and political power. This conflict is mainly articulated in Brutus, an essentially noble and well-intentioned protagonist, whose nobility is bound up with the suppression of feeling and the rigid exclusion of self-knowledge.

It is clear that Cassius' most effective appeal, in the seduction scene (I.ii), is to Brutus' honor, that cultivated selflessness which is, paradoxically, a form of egotism. There are, in the form of Cassius' assault, a number of ironic glances at this self-ignorance in Brutus. And Brutus' initial response to Cassius suggests his failure to grasp either Cassius' meaning or his intentions:

> Into what dangers would you lead me, Cassius,
> That you would have me seek into myself

For that which is not in me?   (I.ii. 63-5)

Does this mean that Brutus, unlike Cassius, is not motivated by envy and hatred? Yes; but it also means (as Cassius will, perhaps inadvertently point out) that Brutus does not *know* what is in him. Disturbed by Cassius' insinuations, Brutus responds obliquely, ambiguously—though he has been, as he says, "with himself at war." Brutus' confusion, his inability to clarify his own motives, is pointed up when Cassius tells him that he will "modestly discover to yourself/That of yourself which you yet know not of."

Of one thing Brutus is fully aware: that his "fear" of Caesar's goals and the "dangers" into which Cassius would lead him conflict with his love for Caesar.[8] He would not have Caesar king; "yet I love him well." And he goes on immediately to declare his love of honor and his patriotism:

> What is it you would impart to me?
> If it be aught toward the general good,
> Set honour in one eye and death i' th' other,
> And I will look on both indifferently;
> For let the gods so speed me as I love
> The name of honour more than I fear death.   (I.ii.84-89)

This juxtaposition epitomizes the moral dilemma of Brutus; and it also conveys his habitual evasion of it. His mind leaps at once to the simple and fastidious code which he understands and can hold fast. He loves Caesar and "the name of honour," and on the horns of that dilemma he will be impaled. For he cannot manage it intellectually; he therefore evades it by pushing it from consciousness and invokes his one sure egoprop: his sense of his own nobility.

A similar process in involved in his persistent attempts to dignify the assassination by giving it a ritual form.[9] This, I think, is the chief significance of Brutus' political mistakes. He is, of course, an ineffective conspirator. But what is thematically more relevant is his *need* to dignify the murder by ritualizing it:

> Let us be sacrificers, but not butchers, Caius.
> We all stand up against the spirit of Caesar,
> And in the spirit of men there is no blood.
> O that we then could come by Caesar's spirit
> And not dismember Caesar! But, alas,
> Caesar must bleed for it!   (II.i.166-71)

The resemblance of this to Othello's "It is the cause, it is the cause . . ." is striking. Othello also regards murder as a kind of sacrifice. Yet the differ-

ence is also noteworthy: Othello believes he is sacrificing Desdemona;
Brutus *wants* to believe the murder of Caesar is sacrificial, but remains
dimly aware of its wrongness. Brutus, in brief, is rationalizing; Othello is
not. There is also an intense irony in Brutus' belief that "in the spirit of
men there is no blood." This glances at the "bloody" motives of the other
conspirators and Brutus' ignorance of those motives. And there is an ironic
rationalization in his "Caesar must bleed for it!" (Compare Othello's "Yet
she must die, else she'll betray more men.") Caesar will bleed indeed, but
his spirit will survive.

That is the brutal import of what occurs just after Brutus' speech to
the populace. Brutus concludes:

> With this I depart, that, as I slew my best lover for the good of
> Rome, I have the same dagger for myself when it shall please my
> country to need my death. (III.ii.51-53)

For the good of Rome, to preserve the people's freedom, he has slain "his
best lover." And then the plebeians shout: "Let him be Caesar. Caesar's
better parts/Shall be crowned in Brutus."[10] The irony does not register in
Brutus' murky soul, but it registers for us. And the recurrent posturing
image ("I have the same dagger . . .") presages the time when he will use his
sword against himself.

A moment later Antony rings (wrings) the changes on "honourable
men," the most honorable of whom is Brutus.[11]

"I know no part of Shakespeare," says Coleridge of the quarrel scene
(IV.iii), "that more impresses on me the belief of his genius being super-
human." He does not go on to explain the power of the scene, and I think
his reticence stems from puzzlement, that the very elements that energize
the scene prevent it from coming readily to the hand of critical analysis.
We are now, I think, in a position to define these elements.

Brutus' second-act soliloquy is, as Virgil Whitaker has noted,[12] a key
passage:

> It must be by his death; and for my part,
> I know no personal cause to spurn at him,
> But for the general. He would be crowned.
> How that might change his nature, there's the question.
> It is the bright day that brings forth the adder,
> And that craves wary walking. Crown him—that!
> And then I grant we put a sting in him
> That at his will he may do danger with.
> Th' abuse of greatness is, when it disjoins

> Remorse from power. And to speak truth of Caesar,
> I have not known when his affections swayed
> More than his reason. But 'tis a common proof
> That lowliness is young ambition's ladder,
> Whereto the climber-upward turns his face;
> But when he once attains the upmost round,
> He then unto the ladder turns his back,
> Looks in the clouds, scorning the base degrees
> By which he did ascend. So Caesar may;
> Then, lest he may, prevent. And since the quarrel
> Will bear no colour for the thing he is,
> Fashion it thus: that what he is, augmented,
> Would run to these and these extremities;
> And therefore think him as a serpent's egg,
> Which, hatched, would as his kind, grow mischievous,
> And kill him in the shell. (II.i.10-34)

It is indeed a crucial moment: Brutus decides to join the conspiracy on the basis of patently fallacious reasoning. This, as Whitaker argues, is Shakespeare's method of making dramatically clear the wrongness of Brutus' decision, and of indicating both its nature and cause. The passage also defines Brutus' essential character: that anomalous combination of moral idealism and intellectual mediocrity, great nobility and dullness of wit.

On the basis of the very insight he thus provides, I must disagree with another judgment of Whitaker's. Early in the quarrel scene Brutus reproves Cassius for his shady methods of getting money. A little later he harshly upbraids him for not sending him money when he asked for it:

> I did send to you
> For certain sums of gold, which you denied me;
> For I can raise no money by vile means.
> By heaven, I had rather coin my heart
> And drop my blood for drachmas than to wring
> From the hard hands of peasants their vile trash
> By any indirection. I did send
> To you for gold to pay my legions,
> Which you denied me. (IV.iii.69-77)

Whitaker finds this passage ineptly written because of Brutus' incredible inconsistency.[13] But Brutus' speech here is, on the contrary, eminently apt. He is nobly contemning the practical means to a desired end—just as he time and again, with fatal consequences, contemns and muddle-headedly rejects the prudent decisions of the more intelligent Cassius. What could more effectively throw up to the mind's eye Brutus' characteristic virtue

and defect than just such inconsistency as he displays here? It is analogous
to the inconsistency Brutus shows in the passage which Whitaker sees as
the key to the play. Brutus' very inconsistency, moreover, implies a hidden
cause for his anger, suggests that there is more reason for his passion than
ever becomes conscious or articulate.

Shortly after Brutus' wrath has strangely and suddenly subsided,
Cassius in wonder remarks: "I did not think you could have been so
angry." Nor did we. Brutus, as we come to know him earlier, is an austere
Stoic, rigidly controlling his passions. His outburst here is not only un-
characteristic; it is clearly excessive in terms of the overt situation. Portia's
death will not suffice as its cause. Her death, in fact, appears to have been
only just thought of, a bit of evidence thrown out to prove that "No man
bears sorrow better." A moment earlier, Brutus cried, "O Cassius, I am
sick of *many* griefs." The death of Portia seems to be the least of them.
The fact is that Brutus himself does not know the cause of his anger. But
we do, or, at any rate, Shakespeare has so managed his scene that we
should. It is there beneath the words, never explicit, because Brutus
cannot know of it.

What is haunting Brutus throughout the scene is the sense of having
committed a horrible and irremediable act: of having murdered his friend
to no purpose. I say this is "haunting" him because he is never consciously
aware of it, never admits or understands the killing as a crime. Unlike
Hamlet and Macbeth, Brutus never achieves self-knowledge; he does not
even attain to the limited self-awareness of Othello. This is but another
aspect of that bluntness of mind which makes his story so poignantly
ironic. He has murdered his "best lover" for what he never ceases to
believe a noble end, for what he never consciously doubts to have been
valid reasons. And he has befriended his worst enemy—could he but see it.
He never knows this, and yet the *feeling* of having committed some ir-
revocable wrong does come to him in the quarrel scene. Though it never
breaches his consciousness, it is there, for him and for us, insistently
asserting itself, tormenting him as only what is unconscious can.

This is why he gives vent to such uncontrollable anger at Cassius. He
never sees that Cassius is his evil spirit, but he senses it. He lashes out at
Cassius without knowing why. He seizes on Cassius' greed, on his refusal to
send him money. Of course, he is inconsistent: *he is attacking his destroyer.* And Brutus is attacking too, perhaps, that dimly-felt and hated aspect
of himself that he can never recognize. In the prelude to the quarrel in
IV.ii, Cassius says (40): "Brutus, this sober form of yours hides wrongs. . . ."
Brutus, in short, is "projecting."

Even while invoking "rational" causes for his anger, Brutus comes
close to the real causes—close enough for us to know what they are.

> Remember March; the ides of March remember.
> Did not great Julius bleed for justice sake?
> What villain touched his body that did stab
> And not for justice?   (IV,iii,18-21)

Only in form are these questions rhetorical. Aside from their irony as addressed to Cassius, they convey Brutus' submerged dubiety, his sense of undefined guilt, in their very assertiveness. And Cassius unwittingly says things that reverberate in the murky and tormented soul of Brutus, where another struggle is going on.

> When Caesar lived he durst not thus have moved me.   (V.iii.58)

> A friend should bear his friend's infirmities,
> But Brutus makes mine greater than they are.   (86-87)

> A friendly eye could never see such faults.   (90)

The quarrel comes to its climax with Cassius' bombastic, plaintive protestation of wounded friendship, and his posturing:

> There is my dagger,
> And here my naked breast; within, a heart
> Dearer than Pluto's mine, richer than gold.
> If that thou be'st a Roman, take it forth.
> I, that denied thee gold, will give my heart.
> Strike as thou didst at Caesar; for I know,
> When thou didst hate him worst, thou lovedst him better
> Than ever thou lovedst Cassius.   (IV.iii.100-7)

Without a moment's pause comes Brutus' "Sheathe your dagger." Why? And why is this sudden, desponding acquiescence so strangely apt? Our answer lies in the speech of Cassius: there the murder of Brutus' other friend has been played out again for him. It is all there—the motive ("If that thou be'st a Roman"), the manner ("here is my naked breast"), the explicit parallel ("Strike as thou didst at Caesar"), the contrast and the climactic truth ("When thou didst hate him worst, thou lovedst him better/Than ever thou lovedst Cassius"). Cassius, unwittingly, has struck home, and his Brutus will never be angry with him again. For Cassius has thus brought to Brutus a profound intimation of his "damnation," a sense of what his high ideals have brought him to, and of the utter futility of ever trying to "justify" himself again. Brutus gives in and gives up:

Be angry when you will; it shall have scope.
Do what you will, dishonour shall be humour. (IV.iii.108-9)

There are no sadder lines in Shakespeare.

We have thus moved to that mood of sad and resigned expectancy
that pervades the rest of the scene. We (and Brutus) await the thing that
remains unspoken, yet hangs in the expectant air. It has not yet taken
form; yet it will come. And we will know it when it comes. This forebod-
ing is implicit even in the tones of the reconciliation—in Cassius' plaintive

O my dear brother,
This was an ill beginning of the night!
Never come such division 'tween our souls!
Let it not, Brutus. (IV.iii.233-36)

and in Brutus' tight-lipped, ambiguous reply: "Everything is well." It is
there too in the sleepy servants—not only the deep, insistent longing of
Brutus for his soul's peace, but the expectancy, enhanced by the servants'
succumbing to sleep and Brutus' lonely watching.

And then Brutus' astonishing tenderness toward his servants:

What, thou speakest drowsily?
Poor knave, I blame thee not; thou art o'erwatch'd....(IV.iii.240-1)

Bear with me, good boy, I am much forgetful.
Canst thou hold up thy heavy eyes awhile,
And touch thy instrument a strain or two? (255-57)

We have not heard these accents from Brutus before, not to Portia. Why
do we hear them now? Because, I think, his profound and inarticulate
suffering has softened the hard egotistical core in him—much as it does to
Lear, except that Lear's suffering is fully conscious and externally imaged.
There has come to Brutus, not knowledge, but an acute sense of his own
scanted humanity, and a fresh sentience to the claims of the heart, whose
neglect has cost him so dearly. This is why his words to Lucius are so
poignant; there is in them not only tenderness, but a deep longing for
peace, for death:

It was well done; and thou shalt sleep again;
I will not hold thee long. If I do live,
I will be good to thee. (IV.iii.264-66)

Do we not feel that the end is soon to come and that, when it comes, it will be welcome?

The boy falls asleep. Brutus reads by the flickering taper. And then what we have been waiting for, what has been haunting Brutus throughout the scene, finally takes form—in the ghost.[14] The ghost "embodies" (if such a word be permitted) the unconscious and virulent guilt that has been tormenting and driving Brutus. The ghost is not merely the ghost of Caesar; it is "Thy evil spirit, Brutus." Even now, though the ghost terrifies him, Brutus does not perceive its meaning. But we do; and that seems to have been what Shakespeare intended.

An unconscious motive. It seems very modern; it seems indeed impossible of dramatic articulation. Yet such a motive is working throughout the scene. Its working explains why critics have been simultaneously dazzled and puzzled by the scene. Brutus' motive *must* be unconscious because the play's peculiar tragic effect—its poignant and pathetic irony—stems in part from Brutus' ignorance about what happens in his own soul. When Brutus speaks to himself, Van Doren remarks, "he knows not who is there; he addresses a strange audience." Yes; and this must be brought home to us. Brutus never comes to know either himself or the scope of his betrayal. "Countrymen," he sums up near the end of the play,

> My heart doth joy that yet in all my life
> I found no man but he was true to me. (V.v.34-35)

And the irony is multifoliate.

Brutus does not seek power as the conspirators do, as Richard III does, as Bolingbroke and his son do. He is indeed an honorable man, one who seeks to perfect his own nature by bringing it into line with what he believes a noble Roman ought to be. He thus embodies a true value. Yet his very nobility is not merely useless to him; it is positively disabling, once he enters the world of politics and power. He is, of course, seduced into that world by the politician, Cassius. Yet it is his "honor" that makes him seducible—that and the "unworldliness" that goes with it.

> If I were Brutus now and he were Cassius,
> He should not humour me. (I.ii.318-19)

Brutus' very idealism blurs his perception of reality. So he never sees, as we do, the irony of the mob's cries that he become another Caesar; and he never sees how he has been used by Cassius. An ultimate irony of the play, furthermore, lies in the fact that Brutus' idealism serves to destroy his destroyer: though the conspirators need Brutus, the conspiracy is fatally compromised by his "nobility."

What remains in our memory of the play is the Brutus who loved Caesar and whose tenderness comes through with such astonishing force in the quarrel scene. And our sense of how little he or the world have made of that tenderness is the basis of the peculiar pathos of his story. That pathos, I suggest, is an expression of the personal theme, of its conflict with and its supremacy over, the Imperial theme. These themes and their opposition were present, vestigially and ambiguously, in the history plays preceding *Julius Caesar*. Here they have come more sharply into focus.

CHAPTER THREE

TROILUS AND CRESSIDA

One reads *Troilus and Cressida* for the first time with mingled shock and bewilderment. Leave *Hamlet* out of our reckoning for the moment, and think of the change of feeling and attitude between *Julius Caesar* (1599) and *Troilus and Cressida* (1602). The difference is astounding. Something has happened to Shakespeare in the interval. The play is not even remotely similar in form to any of the works that precede or succeed it. And we are scarcely prepared for its intense intellectuality.

Yet the play is generally regarded as a crucial one for understanding Shakespeare's work as a whole, a key to Shakespeare's mind. Alas, it is an equivocal sort of key; it is still an open question whether the play is a tragedy, a comical satire, or a farce. Shakespeare's first editors were themselves apparently unsure of its genre, and their puzzlement has a counterpart in criticism of the play right down to the present.[1] The reason lies in the nature of the play itself: it contains apparently contradictory elements which need to be reconciled with each other, if they are not to lead the critic in one false direction or another. I am thinking especially, but not exclusively, of the play's persistent tonal equivocations.[2] From scene to scene, sometimes within a scene, the tone changes abruptly. It is alternately mock-heroic and bathetic, farcical and pathetic, brutally satirical and nearly tragic. Tone is an elusive and hard-to-agree-upon feature of literature; yet its importance in determining attitude and intention will hardly be questioned. And an understanding of the tonal diversity in *Troilus and Cressida* is crucial to an understanding of the play.

Some indications of tone in the play are rather obvious, and the tonal contradictions show up most clearly in connection with them. It will be best to start with these. But even such passages as those we are about to examine have been "subdued" to quite different tonalities by critics who assume that a single tone persists throughout the play.

The tone of the prologue is unequivocally mock-heroic.

> In Troy there lies the scene. From isles of Greece
> The princes orgillous . . .
>   . . . their vow is made
> To ransack Troy, within whose strong immures
> The ravished Helen, Menelaus' queen,
> With wanton Paris sleeps, and *that's the quarrel.*
>   . . . Priam's six-gated city,
> Dardan and Timbria, Helias, Chetas, Troien,
> And Antenorides, with massy staples
> And corresponsive and fulfilling bolts
> Sperr up the sons of Troy.
> Now expectation, *tickling skittish spirits*
> On one and other side, Troyan and Greek,
> Sets all on hazard . . .
>   . . . our play
> Leaps o'er the vaunt and *firstlings of those broils,*
> Beginning in the middle; starting thence away
> To what may be digested in a play.
> Like, or find fault; do as your pleasures are:
> Now good and bad, *'tis but the chance of war.*

The Homeric names and grand phrasing are undercut persistently by abrupt descents into colloquialism (in the phrases I have italicized). The mocking tone is intensified by the prevalence of inkhorn latinisms: "orgillous," "immures," "disgorge," "fraughtage," "corresponsive." The tone is telling us that we are going to see pomposity deflated and pretenses laid bare. It is essentially the tone of satire—though not particularly bitter or serious satire.

The tone of the first scene of the play is, rather obviously, bathetic. Especially as juxtaposed with the mock-heroic tone of the prologue, Troilus' initial speech invites us to laugh, perhaps to snicker, at his love wounds.

> Why should I war without the walls of Troy
> That find such cruel battle here within?
> Each Troyan that is master of his heart,
> Let him to field: Troilus, alas, hath none! (I.i.2-5)

The trite Petrarchan conceit surely mocks the speaker and prevents us from taking Troilus' passion at his own estimate. (If we miss the parodic quality of his speech, we may see Troilus as another Romeo.)[3] In the dialogue with Pandarus that follows, apart from the comic inanity and non-responsiveness of his speech, there is the fact of Pandarus himself, the prototypical pimp, who defines the real nature of Troilus' passion. When Troilus cries out against Pandarus' insensitivity, the brutal images he uses stand out from their Petrarchan matrix:

> I tell thee I am mad
> In Cressid's love. Thou answerest "She is fair"!
> Pourest in the open ulcer of my heart
> Her eyes, her hair, her cheek, her gait, her voice ...
> ....
> But saying thus, instead of oil and balm
> Thou layest in every gash that love hath given me
> The knife that made it.   (I.i.51-54,61-63)

Troilus' passion, though he calls it love, is defined for us by "mad" and "ulcer" and "gash." It is the passion that drives men mad, that ulcerates the heart and gashes the flesh; it is lust. The tone here is established by just this discrepancy between Troilus' delusion and the reality that underlies and belies it. It is a more serious tone than the tone of his initial speech, approaching the bitterly satirical. This is further developed a little later by the juxtaposition of Troilus' frenzied impatience with formulary conceits (I.i.98-103).

There are also passages in the play, related to both the war and the love stories, whose pathetic or near-tragic tone sharply contradicts the tone of the passages we have just examined. There is, first of all, Ulysses' famous speech on degree (I.iii.75-137), whose high seriousness and oratorical dignity will hardly be questioned. It is not, of course, a tragic speech; but its elevated and solemn style is more in accord with a tragic than with a comic context. There is also the Trojan debate scene (II.iii), where the tone is somber, for the lives of many men, indeed the life of a civilization is at stake. However we interpret this scene, its tone cannot be taken as comic or satiric. And then, in the love story, there is that sudden transition to deep, nearly tragic feeling in Troilus' speech when the lovers must part. In its expression of personal loss, it resembles nothing so much as the peculiar eloquence of John Donne:

> We two that with so many thousand sighs
> Did buy each other, must poorly sell ourselves
> With the rude brevity and discharge of one.
> Injurious Time now with a robber's haste
> Crams his rich thievery up, he knows not how.
> As many farewells as be stars in heaven,

> With distinct breath and consigned kisses to them,
> He fumbles up into a loose adieu,
> And scants us with a single famished kiss,
> Distasted with the salt of broken tears. (IV.iv.41-50)

Now, what are we to make of these diversities of tone? (I have thus far left out of account the bawdy and cynical tones of Pandarus and Thersites.) There are, as I see it, two possibilities. We may see the play as mainly satirical—or tragic—with periodic lapses in tonal control. Or we may take the tonal equivocations as intentional: intended to produce a varied but ultimately harmonized set of feelings and attitudes. It is the latter of these possibilities, I think, that squares best with the structure and effect of the play.

Other scenes and passages in the play do not so obviously betray their tones. Particularly difficult in this regard (and crucial to the play's interpretation) are I.iii and III.ii. Many critics take the former of these scenes quite seriously, accepting Agamemnon and Nestor at their own estimate as noble and heroic warriors and making much of Ulysses' speech on degree.[4] There are, however, a number of signs that the tone of the scene is subtly satirical.

There is, first of all, the prolixity, the crammed latinity, and labored syntax of Agamemnon's opening speech:

> Nor, princes, is it matter new to us
> That we come short of our suppose so far
> That after seven years' siege yet Troy walls stand;
> Sith every action that hath gone before
> Whereof we have record, trial did draw
> Bias and thwart, not answering the aim
> And that unbodied figure of the thought
> That gave surmised shape. (I.iii.10-17)

Agamemnon is not so prolix and redundant as Polonius, but he belongs to the same school. He means to say: "This is not the first time we have failed to attain our goal swiftly." Nestor's response, though less knotted in its syntax, is pompous and essentially vacuous. Ulysses, the last to enter an opinion on the issue in question, begins with some fulsome praise of Agamemnon and Nestor (54-69) and concludes with his famous speech on degree—which, as we noted earlier, is serious and eloquent.

If the speeches of Agamemnon and Nestor are satirical (i.e., if they mock the speakers) and Ulysses' speech is not, how are we to construe the tone and intention of the whole scene? A solution lies in seeing the degree speech in relation to its dramatic context. What Ulysses says—that degree is the ladder to all high designs, that "the specialty of rule hath been neglected"—is true. But it applies only ironically to the Greek camp, for there is no one *worthy* of leadership and rule among them. The Greek commanders are all (we see this with increasing clarity in the course of the play) driven by pride and appetite and the lust for power, precisely the motives that Ulysses names as dominant where order and degree are wanting. Where all are equally without merit, there can be no order or degree.

This view of the function of Ulysses' speech is supported in several ways in the same scene. In prefacing his "remedy" for the sickness of the Greek war effort, Ulysses describes Patroclus' mimicry of Agamemnon and Nestor:

> Sometime, great Agamemnon,
> Thy topless deputation he puts on;
> And, like a strutting player—whose conceit
> Lies in his hamstring, and doth think it rich
> To hear the wooden dialogue and sound
> 'Twixt his stretched footing and the scaffolage—
> Such to-be-pitied and o'er-wrested seeming
> He acts thy greatness in; and when he speaks,
> 'Tis like a chime a-mending, with terms unsquared,
> Which, from the tongue of roaring Typhon dropped,
> Would seem hyperboles.   (I.iii.151-61)

His account is so vigorous (and accurate) that it has precisely the reverse effect of what he intends (he means to flatter), and so supports our earlier impression of Agamemnon and Nestor. Furthermore, their very need of Achilles, their implicit recognition that he is in some sort their superior, points up the irony of Ulysses' speech.[5]

The plotting of the Greek leaders is interrupted by the sudden appearance of Aeneas, who comes to speak with Agamemnon, to "Do a fair message to his kingly eyes." Addressing Agamemnon, he asks:

> How may
> A stranger to those most imperial looks
> Know them from eyes of other mortals?   (I.iii.223-25)

The ironic thrust of this is clear; Agamemnon himself sees it: "This Troyan scorns us." And we see that Agamemnon is not distinguishable from other mortals.

The very nature of Ulysses' stratagem, finally, confirms the satiric intention of the scene. Ulysses' views of degree and order hardly square with choosing the best of the Greek warriors by lot—a lot that is fixed so that their best warrior will *not* be chosen. (We see later that only Achilles' personal passion, not Ulysses' "policy," brings Achilles back to the fight.) And the scene ends with Nestor speaking in a style and tone surprisingly like Thersites':

> Ulysses, I begin to relish thy advice . . .
> Two curs shall tame each other. Pride alone
> Must tarre the mastiffs on, as 'twere their bone. (I.iii.388,391-92)

Tonal ambiguities, similar in complexity but dissimilar in their implications, are present in III.ii. Here self-ridicule is articulated *within* some of Troilus' speeches whose tone is basically serious. So that we get a kind of double image of Troilus; we see him both as a self-deluded and lust-ridden fool *and* as a naive, would-be true lover. His first assignation is about to take place; he describes himself thus:

> I stalk about her door
> Like a strange soul upon the Stygian banks
> Staying for waftage. O, be thou my Charon,
> And give me swift transportation to those fields
> Where I may wallow in the lily beds
> Proposed for the deserver! (III.ii.9-14)

The satirical force here derives, not from Petrarchan parody, but from Troilus' comparing his anticipation of Cressida's arms with that of a damned soul awaiting transport to Hades.[6] Whatever Greek notions of the afterlife may have been, an Elizabethan would surely equate Hades with Hell. The sexual meaning of "Hell" is almost certainly operative here also, as in the last line of Sonnet 129. What gives Troilus' speech both a ludicrous and pathetic aspect is just the discrepancy between what he intends and the reality expressed by the figure.

In the much discussed speech that follows ("I am giddy; expectation whirls me round . . ."), it is clear that Troilus' longing is grossly and unequivocally sensual. But it is also clear that he does not know the nature of passion. It is therefore inaccurate to call him "an expert in sensuality" or a "sexual gourmet."[7] And it is also inaccurate to equate his feeling here with the frank desire of Juliet, say, for the sexual consummation of true love. Troilus yearns for pure sensual pleasure. We see that, but Troilus never understands the nature of his yearning.[8] He tries with growing fervor to elevate—to translate—his passion into true love, i.e., into permanence and absoluteness. And this obsessive drive suggests that, below the level of consciousness, Troilus intuits the harsh truth that his passion is in fact transitory and illusory.[9]

The scene we are considering conveys this and much more. After Pandarus' bawdy prelude (III.ii.43-56), the lovers engage in a kind of duet in which what I have been saying about Troilus is brilliantly conveyed, while Cressida's "realistic" view is set off in eloquent contrast.

> *Troilus.* What too curious dreg espies my sweet lady in the fountain of our love?
> *Cressida.* More dregs than water, if my fears have eyes.
> *Troilus.* Fears make devils of cherubins; they never see truly.
> *Cressida.* Blind fear that seeing reason leads, finds safer footing than blind reason stumbling without fear. To fear the worst oft cures the worse.
> *Troilus.* O, let my lady apprehend no fear! In all Cupid's pageant there is presented no monster.
> *Cressida.* Nor nothing monstrous neither? (III.ii.72-82)

It is, we know, a kind of brothel scene. Cressida is aware of this, but Troilus is not. And she is aware, too, of Troilus' delusion.

It has been apparent from the start that Cressida knows what she is about. She is taken in neither by the posturing of warriors nor by the spurious "romantic" protestations of lovers. This is implied by the serious undercurrent in her playful mockery of Pandarus and her deflation of the Greek heroes in I.ii. In the direct speech with which she closes this scene, she makes clear indeed how well she understands the nature of men's love—its nature, at any rate, in the world of the play:

> Yet hold I off. Women are angels, wooing:
> Things won are done; joy's soul lies in the doing.
> That she beloved knows naught that knows not this:
> Men prize the thing ungained more than it is.
> That she was never yet that ever knew
> Love got so sweet as when desire did sue. (I.ii.312-17)

The nature of the "love" implicitly defined here is remarkably similar to the lust explicitly described in Sonnet 129. And, in the world of *Troilus and Cressida*, love is not the only value which is contingent, illusory, subject to time. Cressida's "Men prize the thing ungained more than it is" is echoed later by Troilus' "What is aught but as 'tis valued?" and by Ulysses' "Time hath, my lord, a wallet at his back. . . ." In this world, all values are subject to "envious and calumniating Time," and all the important figures of the play—Ulysses, Troilus, Cressida, Hector, Thersites—more or less clearly see this, though they assume different attitudes toward this central fact of existence.

In the exchange between the lovers in III.ii. Troilus misses Cressida's wry implications (they point to the truth about his passion that he would not admit); but *we* can hardly miss the bitter vision here projected. "Is there nothing monstrous in love?" And Troilus replies:

> Nothing but our undertaking when we vow to weep seas, live in
> fire, eat rocks, tame tigers. . . . This is the monstruosity in love,
> lady, that the will is infinite and the execution confined, that the
> desire is boundless and the act a slave to limit.   (III.ii.83-90)

The passage looks a number of ways at once. Troilus intends to say that he can never adequately express the magnitude of his love. But for us the speech glances sharply at the fatuity of lust-deluded lovers and at the contingency of human love. The double meanings in "will" and "execution" and "act" all refer to the paradox of male sexuality—the very paradox that underlies (again!) Sonnet 129.

> A bliss in proof—and proved, a very woe;
> Before, a joy proposed; behind, a dream.

It is just Troilus' intuition of this that leads him to insist on an impossible transcendence in love and in his beloved.

The sexual allusions in Troilus' speech are picked up by Cressida ("They that have the voice of lions and the act of hares . . .") and, unwittingly, by Troilus:

> Praise us as we are tasted; allow us as we prove. Our head shall
> go bare till merit crown it.   (III.ii.97-99)

A little later Cressida remarks that Troilus is either wise "Or else you love not; for to be wise and love/Exceeds man's might." In reply, Troilus asseverates (this is at once pathetic and satirical) what he would like his mistress to be:

> O that I thought it could be in a woman
> (As, if it can, I will presume in you)
> To feed for aye her lamp and flames of love;
> To keep her constancy in plight and youth
> Outliving beauties outward, with a mind
> That doth renew swifter than blood decays!
> Or that persuasion could but thus convince me,

> That my integrity and truth to you
> Might be affronted with the match and weight
> Of such a winnowed purity in love!
> How were I then uplifted!   (III.ii.165-75)

It is a strange sort of protestation. Troilus does not, and yet he would fain, believe. Can we take him as seriously as the tone suggests we should? Yes; because in a world where love and lust are indistinguishable, where there is nothing but flux, the impulse and the effort to shore up human life against the flux is a serious matter.[10] And so, despite our knowledge of the true nature of Troilus' passion, it is not entirely ironical that, in the ritual assertion of his prototypical status, Troilus should pronounce himself the paradigm of all true lovers (180-189). Nor is it ultimately discordant that the scene should conclude with Pandarus' bawdy obbligato:

> . . . I will show you a chamber with a bed, which, because it
> shall not speak of your pretty encounters, press it to death. Away!
> And Cupid grant all tongue-tied maidens here
> Bed, chamber, Pandar to provide this gear!   (III.ii.214-20)

The Trojan debate (II.ii) is at once the most serious and most puzzling scene of the play. It is, on its face, inconclusive: Hector has the soundest argument, yet he concedes to his sprightly brethren. I think that good dramatic sense can be made of this only if we see the scene in terms that we have been working out for the love story.

The question is: Shall the Trojans keep Helen and continue the war with its terrible consequences? Or shall they give Helen up and end the war? Troilus, the chief spokesman for continuing the war, has several related arguments. Fighting for Helen brings us honor. She is a valuable possession, whose value is certified and enhanced by our fighting for her. Furthermore, having committed ourselves to this cause, it is dishonorable not to stand by our commitment. Hector, on the other side, has two arguments. Helen is not worth what she is costing us. And our cause is morally wrong, since Helen rightly belongs to Menelaus. To persist in "doing wrong extenuates not wrong,/But makes it much more heavy."

Hector clearly has the better of the argument. (His first argument is echoed by Diomedes at IV.i.54-74.) He is the most respectable figure in the play; he knows he is right. Yet he concludes by capitulating:

> Hector's opinion
> Is this in way of truth. Yet ne'ertheless,
> My sprightly brethren, I propend to you

In resolution to keep Helen still;
For 'tis a cause that hath no mean dependence
Upon our joint and several dignities. (II.ii.188-94)

To attribute Hector's capitulation to weakness of will, as Tillyard does, is surely a mistake: Hector is obviously the strongest-willed of the Trojans.[11] To maintain, as Nevill Coghill does, that Hector's argument is false because Helen doesn't wish to return to her husband, and that Hector sees the weakness of his position—this seems downright perverse.[12] Our only reasonable inference must be that Hector also perceives that nothing is either good or bad but thinking makes it so.

In this respect, the war story parallels the love story, and Hector's final position precisely parallels Troilus'.[13] Hector argues from the ground of reason—either practical reason or theoretical—and so we cannot help but see that his argument is much stronger than Troilus'. But in the world of the play reason is no longer the arbiter of right action, any more than the idea of degree is the true model of the social and political order. "Nay," says Troilus,

> if we talk of reason
> Let's shut our gates, and sleep. Manhood and honour
> Should have hare hearts, would they but fat their thoughts
> With this crammed reason. (II.ii.46-49)

When Hector remarks, with hard practical sense, that Helen "is not worth what she doth cost/The holding," Troilus replies: "What is aught but as 'tis valued?" Having seen the way "crammed reason" is used by Ulysses, we may find ourselves sympathizing here with Troilus. We can understand, in any case, why he "elevates" Cressida and Helen into pearls of price. If Cressida is unworthy of true love, if no woman is worthy of it, one must create value by willing and acting. At I.i.114-15 Troilus accurately estimates Helen's worth. Yet here he speaks of her as a pearl "Whose price hath launched above a thousand ships/And turned crowned kings to merchants." Helen's value is a function of what has been done for her. It may, as Hector says, "be mad idolatry/To make the service greater than the god"; but where there are no gods, idolatry is preferable to nothing.

This is why, despite Cassandra's warnings and his own good sense, Hector later replies to Ulysses' prediction that Troy must fall:

> I must not believe you.
> There they stand yet; and modestly I think
> The fall of every Phrygian stone will cost
> A drop of Grecian blood. The end crowns all,

> And that old common arbitrator, Time,
> Will one day end it.   (IV.v.221-26)

Hector must not believe, as Troilus must not believe, what he knows to be true, because time will destroy all: love and honor and war and life itself. And so, what modicum of value is possible must be created and held fast, no matter what it costs the keeping. This is the faith that Hector must not, cannot, break. Thus, at the end (V.ii) he rejects the pleas of Andromache, Cassandra, and Priam and goes to what he must know is certain death. His response to all entreaty is: "I must not break my faith."

This is the view of the human condition which underlies Ulysses' eloquent arguments to Achilles:

> Let not virtue seek
> Remuneration for the thing it was!
> For beauty, wit,
> High birth, vigour of bone, desert in service,
> Love, friendship, charity, are subject all
> To envious and calumniating Time.   (III.iii.169-74)

Nothing lasts. Everything changes, everything is subject to time. And so nothing can be said to really *be*. If he longs for value and permanence, man's only recourse, whether in love or war, is to pursue a never-to-be-attained shadow of transcendence. That is not much, but that is all there is.

This is why, though he is persistently ridiculed in the play, Troilus can yet be taken seriously. He is not, as Cressida sees, a true lover. But that does not make his yearning for such status, his need for transcendence, less respectable. When the lovers part, therefore, it is not surprising to find in Troilus' speech (IV.iv.41-50) the most nearly tragic verse in the play. In the passage that follows this, Troilus repeatedly urges Cressida to be true. As she perceives, his insistence betrays his own lack of faith; it also indicates his intuitive grasp of the reality of their situation. "O heavens! you love me not," she says, and she is partly right. But, however she may change, Troilus will remain true, as he prophesies. He must be true, not to her exactly, but to his self-born image of love.

When, in the same scene, Troilus gives his love (symbolically and literally) into the hands of Diomedes, we can foretell the issue. For we know that Diomedes is, like Cressida, a realist, one who sees clearly the worthlessness of Helen and the idiocy of the war. When Troilus warns him to use Cressida well, Diomedes replies with prophetic irony:

> When I am hence,
> I'll answer to my lust; and know you, lord,
> I'll nothing do on charge. To her own worth
> She shall be prized . . . (IV.iv.133-36)

And so, indeed, she is. It is not quite fair to call her a daughter of the game. In her way she loves Troilus more than he loves her. But she is one who knows the power of envious time, knows it is a world where men will never tarry. And she makes the best of it. Since men will prize her at her own worth, she must accommodate herself—because her worth depends, paradoxically, on how they prize her.

But Troilus, like Hector in his own way, cannot accommodate himself as Cressida "realistically" does. Watching Cressida betray him, Troilus will not believe his own eyes. "This she? No, this is Diomed's Cressida!" From one point of view, Troilus' behavior is ludicrous, absurd. From another (his own), it is quite logical. For the Cressida who betrays him is *Diomedes'* Cressida: she *is* what he desires her to be. She is therefore not *Troilus'* Cressida. And so he can say—ludicrously? seriously?—

> Hark, Greek! As much as I do Cressid love,
> So much by weight hate I her Diomed. (V.ii.167-68)

Troilus still loves *his* Cressida. And so he is at once quite rational and absurd in fighting, as the Trojans fight for a worthless Helen, for a worthless Cressida.

To illustrate the pervasive Thersites motif, the following may serve:[14]

> That dissembling abominable varlet, Diomed, has got that same
> scurvy doting foolish young knave's sleeve of Troy there in his
> helm. I would fain see them meet, that that same young Troyan
> ass that loves the whore there, might send that Greekish whore-
> masterly villain with the sleeve back to the dissembling luxurious
> drab of a sleeveless errand. O' the t'other side, the policy of those
> crafty swearing rascals—that stale old mouse-eaten dry cheese,
> Nestor, and that same dog-fox, Ulysses—is not proved worth a
> blackberry. They set me up, in policy, that mongrel cur Ajax
> against that dog of as bad a kind, Achilles; and now is the cur
> Ajax prouder than the cur Achilles . . . (V.iv.2-15)

The extraordinary thing about Thersites is that the vision he expresses is simultaneously revolting and true. Otherwise clear-sighted critics nevertheless persistently dismiss him. "Nobody in the play," says Kittredge, "takes him seriously. His satirical comments upon the Grecian and the Trojan heroes do not express Shakespeare's opinion, nor would any Elizabethan audience have taken them in that sense."[15] And Tillyard says:

> To make Thersites into a chorus, the authentic commentator on the play's action, is ridiculous. His function is that of a Fool, to give a twist to every action and every motive. And this twist is always to the vile and the loathsome. Sometimes he hits the mark, at others, he is wide of it.[16]

But from one standpoint in this many-faceted play, everything Thersites says is true. That he plays the fool is surely no guarantee that he is not an authentic commentator, nor indeed is the fact that his view of things is vile and loathsome. The critics' reluctance to accept Thersites' view of things (and he almost always hits the mark) is itself a clue to Shakespeare's intentions. Thersites' vision (and Thersites himself) are simply too revolting to be accepted. Thus, like Troilus, we recoil from that vision, and seek to create another truth, one that makes our world bearable. Thus our natural reaction to Thersites reinforces the meaning that I have been urging as the central meaning of the play.

If Thersites tells us how things really are, Pandarus, who neither sees nor tells us much, *embodies* that reality. He has no distinct personality; he is rather a locus of indistinct and uncontrolled feeling—largely erotic feeling. He is what a human being would be without a mind or a will. Having, as it were, no self, Pandarus becomes by sheer empathy whoever he is in contact with. In III.ii he is not merely an efficient pimp; he identifies with both Troilus and Cressida and enjoys himself in some perversely erotic way:

> Come, come, what need you blush? Shame's a baby,— Here she is now. Swear the oaths now to her that you have sworn to me.— What, are you gone again? You must be watched ere you be made tame, must you? Come your ways, come your ways. An you draw backward, we'll put you i' th' fills. Why do you not speak to her? Come, draw this curtain and let's see your picture. Alas the day, how loath you are to offend daylight! An 'twere dark, you'ld close sooner . . . (III.ii.42-52)

Early in the play (I.ii.85) Pandarus tells Troilus: "I would my heart were in her body!" That was not, it appears, a figure of speech. Now his heart is in both their bodies.[17]

In view of the diversity of tones in the play and the consequent appearance of contradictory intentions, it is not surprising that critics have found the play hard to classify. Yet this very tonal equivocation appears to convey, rather powerfully I think, a coherent vision of the sort I have tried to describe. The play is therefore neither a tragedy nor a comical satire, but a genre for which we have no name. Its main effect is one of bitter revulsion and hopeless stoicism. This is why the satirical view of the play proposed by O. J. Campbell seems to me as much an over-simplification as the purely tragic view. Tillyard never makes quite clear his view of the play's nature. In some ways my view comes close to his. But he insists that "the old interpretation of the play as an outburst of unrestrained bitterness against life, to be overcome later, is fantastically false."[18] And Nevill Coghill sees the play as "a tragic contemplation of the overthrow of a great tradition typified by two high secular ideals . . . good faith and clear honor in war and love."[19]

But the play itself envisions the world as a meaningless chaos, to which one may respond in various ways, none of them really adequate. One may accommodate oneself by swaying with the wind, surviving as best one can—as Cressida does—or by manipulating the flux—as Ulysses does (though his policy is proved not worth a blackberry). One may rail with Thersites or immerse oneself in pure feeling with Pandarus. But the most respectable response to such a world—the most noble, though ultimately fatuous—is the response of Troilus and Hector.[20] Each in his own way attempts to create value where value does not and cannot exist. Each attempts to act as though value were possible—though they both know that that old common arbitrator time will one day end all. That is the bleak vision which is in large measure articulated by the diverse, apparently contradictory tones of the play.

CHAPTER FOUR

OTHELLO

Desdemona, G. Wilson Knight observes, is at once Othello's "divinity" and a warmly human creature; she is "to be equated with the divine principle," yet there is "a certain domestic femininity about her."[1] Knight does not explain how Desdemona comes to have this dual status; yet such status she does possess. This is, indeed, but one of several "dualities" that distinguish the play's style and effect and help to keep its critics at bay.

Even our initial impression of *Othello* is oddly contradictory: we get, on the one side, a sense of classical neatness and clarity; on the other, a sense of intentions not quite realized. The source of this impression, I think, is the play's use of two divergent expressive modes, two styles that our usual canons of taste find incompatible. This is not a matter merely of tonal equivocation of the sort we found in *Troilus and Cressida*, and there is never any question about the high seriousness of the play. The "impurity" of style, moreover, is not expressive of contradictory attitudes; it serves rather to present the action of the play on two different "levels" and to express two kinds of meaning more or less simultaneously.

The notion of stylistic impurity in Elizabethan drama is, of course, not new.[2] But the *kind* of impurity we find in *Othello* differs from that to be found in Webster and has not, so far as I know, been described. The most prominent example of it is the equivocal use to which Shakespeare puts the "primitive" dramatic conventions with which Schücking has familiarized us. When Othello says, "Not I, I must be found./My parts, my title, and my perfect soul/Shall manifest me rightly," he is to be taken at his word. His speech has its "face value" as a directly characterizing unnaturalistic device. Yet his speech is not *merely* direct; it is also indirectly "naturally" characterizing. Thus, the main impression we get of Othello is the one Samuel Johnson describes: "magnanimous, artless, and credulous, boundless in his confidence, ardent in his affection." But that impression is undercut by a contradictory impression of self-deluding, childlike egotism. Both impressions are valid, both are rooted in the play. And what makes this possible is Shakespeare's equivocal method of characterization.

A similar method is used in the characterization of Iago, to whom we shall come presently. Let me now only emphasize that in presenting his protagonist Shakespeare merges two diverse dramatic modes. A critic unaware of this is likely to find the play contradictory in some respects. For he may attend to the signs of the noble Othello and neglect the egotistical one; or he may do just the reverse. In either case, he will run up against contradiction. Now, if the two Othellos are not in fact contradictory, if the two modes of dramatic expression just described serve rather to create an integral, coherent drama, then I think we must assume that there is more than one level of action and meaning in the play.

There are, I believe, two distinct levels of action and meaning in the play. There is a natural, "domestic" action; and there is a supernatural, or transcendent, or quasi-theological action. On the *natural* level the action involves the wanton destruction of a noble and simple-souled man by a motiveless yet ineluctable malignity, the gratuitous destruction of love by an envious and loveless rationalist. The *supernatural* action depends on the natural, even as it transcends it. In ways that I shall try to explain, Othello becomes for us a representative man, an Everyman. His love, though tainted like every man's with self-love, becomes a means of self-transcendence, a poetic equivalent of faith. Desdemona becomes a kind of divinity; Iago a diabolical force; and Othello's succumbing to Iago is his "damnation."

Iago clearly operates on both levels. He is an embittered, malcontent soldier; emotionally crippled, incapable of love, he is therefore envious of lovers and compelled to destroy love. He is also an embodiment of the ineradicable evil in nature and of the malevolence in human nature. (In a peripheral way, he also serves as a "projector" of the egotistic tendency of Othello himself, an image of this natural human impulse raised to the level of monstrosity.)

These different kinds of action and meaning are both derived from a *literal* interpretation of the play. That is to say: they are not derived by the use of different *methods* of interpretation, of the sort that Dante prescribes for the interpretation of his *Commedia*. Their differentiation is a consequence, rather, of the *real presence* of two distinct expressive modes in the play.

In presenting the natural action, Shakespeare had to face the problem of credibility. How can the violent jealousy of so noble and trusting a man as Othello be made convincing? This is the issue that has obsessed rationalistic critics of the play since Rymer. Yet it is clear that Shakespeare has solved the problem; it is clear, at any rate, once we discern the two kinds of action in the play. Shakespeare has, for one thing, given extraordinary care to the delineation of Iago's character and to impressing upon us Iago's ability to deceive and manipulate others. In the first scene of the play, we see Iago in action, leading Roderigo by the nose. What is curious about this scene is this: Iago displays a virtuosity far greater than the case requires. Roderigo is a "snipe," a fool. He cannot see that Iago's description of himself means that Roderigo is being used, is Iago's dupe. This is sometimes taken as an indication of Iago's delight in his own powers; but this seems to me too "realistic" an inference. The effect of Iago's excessive display is twofold: we are impressed with Iago's mastery, but, more important, we surmise a level of action and meaning other than the natural one. Since Iago, in any case, deceives everyone in the play, we cannot question his ability to deceive Othello—especially an Othello who is not only noble and trusting, but whose nobility is inseparable from a kind of naive egotism which makes him particularly vulnerable to Iago's lies.

And then there is the curious "goodness" of Desdemona, a goodness ambiguous in the dramatic context, for it assists in her own destruction. Iago explains it for us:

> ... by how much she strives to do him good,
> She shall undo her credit with the Moor.
> So will I turn her virtue into pitch,
> And out of her own goodness make the net
> That shall enmesh them all.   (II.iii.364-68)

Precisely this process is dramatized in one of the most terrible scenes in the play. It comes after Othello's "fall," after Iago's poison has penetrated Othello's mind and heart. Terrified by Othello's, to her, inexplicable rage, Desdemona still struggles to keep her promise to Cassio, her "honesty" thus "proving" her infidelity:

Oth.	Fetch't, let me see 't!
Des.	Why, so I can, sir; but I will not now.
	This is a trick to put me from my suit.
	Pray you, let Cassio be received again.
Oth.	Fetch me the handkerchief! my mind misgives.
Des.	Come, come!
	You'll never meet a more sufficient man.
Oth.	The handkerchief!

Des.   A man that all his time
              Hath founded his good fortunes on your love,
              Shared dangers with you—
Oth.   The handkerchief!   (III.iv.86-96)

In the willow scene (IV.ii) we get a similar vision—a more poignant one—of virtue too fine for survival in a gross and imperfect world. Presaging her imminent death, Desdemona's mind turns to apparently irrelevant fancies. "This Ludovico is a proper man." Ludovico is a cultivated Venetian, the sort of man she would have married in the ordinary course of events, the sort of man she would have married if she had been more prudent and less pure of heart. "Dost thou in conscience think—tell me, Emilia—/That there be women do abuse their husbands/In such gross kind?" She cannot conceive of such things—so innocent (in two senses) is she. Emilia knows that such things do indeed occur. And perhaps only half-seriously, she tells Desdemona that she herself might do it if the price were right. "The world's a huge thing; it is a great price/For a small vice." The contrast between the two women could not be more brilliantly articulated or more apt. We see that Desdemona would not be on the verge of destruction if she were only more like the grosser-souled and more sophisticated Emilia. Yet we also see that if she were more like Emilia, she would not be Desdemona.

Othello's character, too, is such (as we have already noted) as to facilitate Iago's task. He is psychologically vulnerable; and he is "of a free and open nature,/That thinks men honest that but seem to be so." Given such a victim, such a wife, and such a villain, it seems mere captiousness to question the probability of Iago's enmeshing them all. On the natural level, the play has as much probability as any of the tragedies.

By the naturalistic method of characterization, we are given to see the unconscious substratum of the Othello who is nonetheless noble and heroic. This dual vision of Othello (not the split one) accounts, I think, for the persistent division between critics who see only the outward man and those who see only the inner one. An understanding of Shakespeare's method, however, should lead rather to an imaginative grasp of Othello as a complex but integral personality. Furthermore, it is just by way of our perception of the paradox of his personality—nobility rooted in egotism, egotism rooted in nobility—that we begin to see a meaning beyond the particular and the natural. When the roots of his personality are exposed to view, Othello's individuality and the extraordinary aspects of his situation fall away. The play begins to take on a *general* and *supernatural* meaning.

Othello becomes Everyman (while he also remains his individual self), because every man has in him the very tendencies and passions that are uncovered in the barbaric, strange, and exotic Moor. In this way the quasi-theological meaning of the play is included in the natural one—though they remain distinct meanings. Because we know that there is an inner and an outward self—a conscious and an unconscious—there is no real contradiction between the one Othello and the other. Not all men are as noble as Othello, or as simple, or as naive. Not all men marry as lovely a person as Desdemona, or are subject to the machinations of an Iago. Yet all men have in them the seeds of passion, the ineradicable egotism, the proneness to self-doubt that we find in Othello. These are the traits that lead men to love, that underlie their need to be loved; and they are also the causes of love's death. They exist universally, in the best as in the worst of men.

I have already described the double effect of the protagonist's direct, self-characterizing speeches. Another illustration may be in order. Here is Othello's first long speech:

> Let him do his spite.
> My services which I have done the signiory
> Shall outtongue his complaints. 'Tis yet to know—
> Which, when I know that boasting is an honour,
> I shall promulgate—I fetch my life and being
> From men of royal siege; and my demerits
> May speak (unbonneted) to as proud a fortune
> As this that I have reached. For know, Iago,
> But that I love the gentle Desdemona,
> I would not my unhoused free condition
> Put into circumscription and confine
> For the sea's worth. (I.ii.17-28)

Apart from the direct statement of his nobility and the indirect implication of his egotism, there is also something very difficult to describe: a pervasive, sonorous grandiloquence which bespeaks a soul at once grand and childlike, simple and sensuous, self-obsessed yet deficient in self-knowledge. I refer, of course, to what Knight calls the "Othello music" in an essay of great brilliance.[3]

I do not wish to suggest that Othello's egotism is a moral flaw. In the fictive world of the play, it is at once an imperfection in his nature and a concomitant of his virtue, his nobility. It is just this concomitance that makes it an emphatic sign of the egotism of human nature: of the self-love which roots all human action and is an ineluctable presence in human love. "She loved me for the dangers I had passed,/And I loved her that she did pity them." Othello falls in love, not (as Cinthio has it) because he is "conquered by [Desdemona's] beauty and nobility of mind," but because she admires his soldiership, the basis of his self-esteem. It is just this taint that makes him, for all his trustfulness, vulnerable to Iago. And he is vulnerable precisely to the degree that his love is grounded, not on the lovableness of the beloved, but on self-love.

This is not to deny that he loves Desdemona. He loves her deeply—in the only way it is in his nature to love: pathetically ignorant of the sacrifice of selfhood that loving truly demands of the lover. This is made clear enough in the play. After the initial difficulties of his marriage have been resolved, he assures the Venetian Senate that his love will never interfere with his serious business:

> And heaven defend your good souls that you think
> I will your serious and great business scant
> For she is with me. No, when light-winged toys
> Of feathered Cupid seel with wanton dullness
> My speculative and officed instruments,
> That my disports corrupt and taint my business,
> Let housewives make a skillet of my helm,
> And all indign and base adversities
> Make head against my estimation!   (I.iii.267-75)

Light-winged toys, indeed! The man does not know what love is or what it means; that is the vicious mole in his particular nature. And there is a mordant irony in his confident protestation, for his "disports" do indeed corrupt and taint his business, and when they do, his "estimation" is utterly shattered.

His contempt for love, his confident belief that love is but a toy, is first shaken in the temptation scene. Before Iago sets to work, his victim is unwittingly softened up, made more than ordinarily vulnerable, by Desdemona. In pleading for Cassio, she is interfering in Othello's professional affairs, corrupting and tainting his business. Othello is so unnerved by this (for him) new experience, that he is off balance just when Iago makes his assault. At first Othello resists, as he should, the demand of his love that he sacrifice his judgment in an official matter. But Desdemona is ignorantly and virtuously insistent:

> What? Michael Cassio,
> That came a-wooing with you, and so many a time,
> When I have spoke of you dispraisingly,
> Hath ta'en your part—to have so much to do
> To bring him in? Trust me, I could do much—(III.iii.70-74)

Her voice is the voice of feeling, of love. Othello responds to its call, but only after overcoming intense inner resistance. "Prithee no more. Let him come when he will!/I will deny thee nothing." Even this is not enough for Desdemona; she hammers away at him. "I will deny thee nothing," he cries again. Now he is really shaken: he has felt for the first time the awful power of love, and it has interfered with his soldiership. Watching Desdemona depart, he gets a dark intimation of the terrible consequences of his "enslavement" in the confused passion which the moment calls up in him:

> Excellent wretch! Perdition catch my soul
> But I do love thee! and when I love thee not,
> Chaos is come again. (III.iii.90-92)

He is discovering something utterly new to him. His naive belief in his self-sufficiency has come up against the actuality of his counterpoised love and dependence on Desdemona. And in his sudden awareness of that dependence, he also senses the fragility of his strength and confidence. It is just when he is thus deeply shaken that he is assaulted by the rationalistic and loveless Iago. Is it unlikely that he should then listen to Iago's voice?

The pattern I have been tracing is developed later in the temptation scene, when Othello tells Iago (with now hollow-sounding confidence):

> Thinkest thou I'ld make a life of jealousy,
> To follow still the changes of the moon
> With fresh suspicions? No! To be once in doubt
> Is once to be resolved . . . .
> . . . on the proof there is no more but this—
> Away at once with love or jealousy! (III.iii.177-180;192-93)

To which we get, a moment later, his emphatically ironic response, his formal farewell to his profession and his happiness:

> O, now forever
> Farewell the tranquil mind! farewell content!
> Farewell the plumed troop, and the big wars
> That make ambition virtue! (347-50)

It is one of the most poignant speeches in the play. And it, too, is equivocal: his words are simply true, yet his magniloquence conveys his failure to realize fully what he is losing forever.

The theological action and meaning of the play are most emphatically articulated by a dramatic mode that is easily missed if one is not prepared for it. I call it—for want of a better term—"operatic." It involves an abrupt cessation of the naturalistic action, a sudden transition to stylized or formalized action, conveyed by way of juxtaposed, patterned "parts" or "songs." In effect, we are suddenly translated to another kind of reality, to a fictive world where human relations are expressed by formal patterns outside time, and where thought, feeling, and character are presented by formal "parts" rather than "natural" speech.

The most notable instance of this occurs in the first scene of act II. The scene begins naturalistically with the apprehensive watching for Othello's ships. With the arrival of Desdemona, we get a momentary shift into the operatic mode. There is a ritualistic quality to the welcome she receives; while she stands graciously receiving their homage, everyone kneels, and Cassio speaks (sings?) for them all:

> O, behold!
> The riches of the ship is come on shore!
> Ye men of Cyprus, let her have your knees.
> Hail to thee, lady! and the grace of heaven,
> Before, behind thee, and on every hand,
> Enwheel thee round!   (II.i.82-87)

The action returns again to the naturalistic mode. While we wait for Othello's ship, Desdemona masks her anxiety by engaging in witty banter with Iago. Despite the lightness of tone here, there is a current of serious implication, a nasty ambiguity in Iago's mock-serious misogyny. This is especially notable in his reply to Desdemona's "What wouldst thou write of me, if thou shouldst praise me?" "O gentle lady," he says, "do not put me to it;/ For I am nothing, if not critical."

Then, while Cassio engages Desdemona in courtly conversation, we get an aside from Iago:

> He takes her by the palm. Ay, well said, whisper! With as little
> a web as this will I ensnare as great a fly as Cassio. Ay, smile upon
> her, do! I will gyve thee in thine own courtship. . . .   (II.i.168-72)

The speech has a naturalistic status; and as such it convey Iago's malice and envy with great eloquence. But it also has the status of a kind of recitative, a kind of formal announcement of events to come. As a result, the naturalistic action disappears, and we enter a world outside of time, in which the diabolical manipulator tells us what he has in store for the unsuspecting couple across the stage. It is not merely "exposition." Iago's aside establishes the scene as a tableau, a timeless image of the supernatural reality which is one of the play's chief meanings. It is also a prelude to what immediately follows.

The Iago motif, a recurrent one, is set sharply against Desdemona's song of love and Othello's peculiar music. Iago's theme is the nasty vision of love as bestiality: "Yet again your fingers to your lips? Would they were clyster pipes for your sake!" This harsh dissonance leads into the harmonious "duet" between the newly-arrived Othello and Desdemona.

> *Oth.*   O my fair warrior!
> *Des.*   My dear Othello!
> *Oth.*   It gives me wonder great as my content
>   To see you here before me. O my soul's joy!
>   If after every tempest come such calms,
>   May the winds blow till they have wakened death!
>   And let the labouring bark climb hills of seas
>   Olympus-high, and duck again as low
>   As hell's from heaven! If it were now to die,
>   'Twere now to be most happy; for I fear
>   My soul hath her content so absolute
>   That not another comfort like to this
>   Succeeds in unknown fate.
> *Des.*   The heavens forbid
>   But that our loves and comforts should increase
>   Even as our days do grow!
> *Oth.*   Amen to that, sweet powers!
>   I cannot speak enough of this content:
>   It stops me here; it is too much of joy.
>   And this, and this, the greatest discords be
>   That e'er our hearts shall make!   (II.i.184-201)

This passage may be read naturalistically. Othello's wonder at his own joy, his hyperboles, and the general grandeur of his rhetoric suggest the latent egotism, the engrossment in passion, and the underlying sensuality which is involved in his love for Desdemona. His speeches here are somewhat similar in their import to the utterances of Troilus (another self-deluding lover) while he anticipates the consummation of his passion.[4] But the passage is also operatic in mode. There are clear signs of it: the pause in outward action, the melodiousness of the speeches, the climactic access of lyric feeling, the reverberating implications. There is, further, the explicit "pointing" of Iago's aside, which immediately follows the love duet: "O you are well tuned now!/But I'll set down the pegs that make this music,/As honest as I am."

Considered thus, the passage carries other meanings, the ones I have called quasi-theological. G. Wilson Knight describes the passage with fine precision, though in somewhat different terms than the ones we have been using, thus:

Othello, Desdemona, and their love are here apparent, in this scene of storm and reverberating discharge of cannon, as things of noble and conquering strength: they radiate romantic valour. Othello is essential man in all his prowess and protective strength; Desdemona essential woman, gentle, loving, brave in trust of her warrior husband. The war is over. The storm of sea or bruit of cannonade are powerless to hurt them: yet there is another storm brewing in the venomed mind of Iago. . . . The scene is thus a microcosm of the play, reflecting its action. Colours which are elsewhere softly toned are here splashed vividly on the play's canvas. Here especially Othelllo appears a prince of heroes, Desdemona is lit by a divine feminine radiance: both are transfigured. They are shown as coming safe to land, by Heaven's 'grace,' triumphant, braving war and tempestuous seas, guns thundering their welcome.[5]

It is precisely the operatic mode that thus images and expresses the theological meaning of the play. (This is why the mode is timeless, separated from ordinary reality.) Othello has found (to use our own terms) in Desdemona's love a fulfillment of his soul's deepest need—an analogue of salvation, if you will. And we see that Iago, the egotistic-rationalistic principle in human nature, stands in love's path, waiting for the moment he is sure will come when he can turn love into hatred, "salvation" into "damnation."

The presence of theological meanings in the play is suggested by persistent use of theological terms by various speakers in the play. A few instances:

> Hell and night
> Must bring this monstrous birth to the world's light. (I.iii.408-9)

> . . . letting go safely by
> The divine Desdemona. (II.i.72-73)

> Divinity of hell!
> When devils will the blackest sins put on,
> They do suggest at first with heavenly shows,
> As I do now. (II.iii.356-59)

> Perdition catch my soul
> But I do love thee! (III.iii.90-91)

> When we shall meet at compt,
> This look of thine will hurl my soul from heaven,
> And fiends will snatch at it. (V.iii.286)

The theological level of action and meaning is articulated by another device, one that serves to keep before the mind theological implications at moments when they might be submerged and forgotten. It is a kind of ironically reverberating utterance which carries meanings beyond the natural ones which ground the irony. We have an instance of the usual ironic method in Othello's "If after every tempest come such calms,/ Let the winds blow till they have wakened death!" or "If it were now to die,/ 'Twere now to be most happy. . . . " Here we get a prediction of the future which is true, but whose truth is unknown and unintended by the speaker. The kind of utterance I am trying to describe is not predictive, but it is true in several ways at once, and it emphatically articulates transcendent or theological meanings. It reverberates.

There is a good example in the first scene of the play. In the course of his remonstration with Roderigo, Iago increasingly addresses the audience, until he virtually speaks to them alone, and Roderigo is all but forgotten:

> Heaven is my judge, not I for love and duty,
> But seeming so, for my peculiar end;
> For when my outward action does demonstrate
> The native act and figure of my heart
> In compliment extern, 'tis not long after
> But I will wear my heart upon my sleeve
> For daws to peck at. *I am not what I am.* (I.i.59-65)

The final clause summarizes the thought of the passage: Iago serves himself, not the Moor. But it means more than this. It means that he is not what he appears to be to Roderigo, *or to us.* It means—this is what reverberates—that he is not even what he *is*: a soldier, a man, a fictive creature of the play; that he is rather (something that nearly escapes definition) a creature beyond the natural order and so supernatural, inhuman. *"I am not what I am."*

Sometimes the method is at once ironic and transcendent in effect. In I.iii Brabantio warns Othello: "Look to her, Moor, if thou hast eyes to see;/She has deceived her father, and may thee." And, speaking a truth he cannot know, in words that signify theologically, Othello replies: "My life upon her faith!" And is there not a transcendent meaning in the words that follow? "Honest Iago,/My Desdemona must I leave to thee."

In the temptation scene (III.iii), after the first, slight doubt (the breach in his faith which insures his "damnation"), Othello utters this innocuous and formulary phrase to his destroyer: "I am bound to thee forever." The phrase reverberates: He *is* Iago's now, he is Iago's *forever.* And at the very end of the scene, Othello, now utterly "lost," tells Iago: "Now art thou my lieutenant." And Iago replies, smirking, echoing and varying Othello's earlier phrase: *"I am your own forever."* They are now inhabitants of the same world; they now belong, in a sense, to each other. And the world they inhabit is the world of forever, outside of time. It is Hell.

The diverse styles of the play do not stand in one-to one correspondence with the two levels of action and meaning. Rather, the natural and supernatural meanings are more or less present throughout the play—though they do receive different degrees of emphasis at this moment or that. When, for example, Iago gives Roderigo his estimate of the marriage, he does so in naturalistic prose:

> Her eye must be fed; and what delight shall she have to look on
> the devil? When the blood is made dull with the act of sport, there
> should be, again to inflame it, and to give satiety a fresh appetite,
> loveliness in favour, sympathy in years, manners, and beauties; all
> which the Moor is defective in. Now, for want of these required
> conveniences, her delicate tenderness will find itself abused, begin
> to heave the gorge, disrelish and abhor the Moor. Very nature will
> instruct her in it and compel her to some second choice. (II.i.227-38)

Iago is not only trying to keep up Roderigo's hopes; he also *means* what he says. And his compulsion thus to envision human love as bestial suggests his status as both an emotionally crippled rationalist and an embodiment of evil. It is in terms of both his perverse psychology and his satanic status that Iago can be understood to "love" Desdemona—"not out of absolute lust," as he tells us—but out of his suprapersonal need to turn virtue to pitch, to dominate, to possess, and to destroy.

In more formal passages, we find a similar doubleness of meaning. We find it in Iago's soliloquy toward the end of act II:

> And what's he then that says I play the villain,
> When this advice is free I give and honest,
> Probal to thinking and indeed the course
> To win the Moor again? . . .
> His soul is so enfettered to her love,
> That she may make, unmake, do what she list,
> Even as her appetite shall play the god
> With his weak function. How am I then a villain
> To counsel Cassio to this parallel course,
> Directly to his good? Divinity of hell!
> When devils will the blackest sins put on,
> They do suggest at first with heavenly shows,
> As I do now. . . . (II.iii.342-45;351-59)

Iago knows well one side of Othello: he speaks truly when he says that Othello's soul is "enfettered" to Desdemona's love. This is the natural insight of the egotist into the soul of another with whom he has some affinity, however slight. It is, of course, "unnatural" for Iago thus directly to address the audience, to discuss his fictive role with them. But this apparent destruction of dramatic illusion has its function. By thus stepping outside himself, Iago signifies his supernatural status. That is, by calling in question his *fictive* reality, he achieves a kind of super-reality in the world of the play. And that earlier phrase reechoes: *"I am not what I am."*

I think it is clear that *Othello* is not the rather unambiguous moral play that Leavis concludes it to be.[6] Both its natural and supernatural action articulate a vision of human love and human life that is grimly pessimistic beyond anything else in Shakespeare's work. Othello remains, if not guiltless, not clearly sinful. He is the noble man in a situation beyond his ken and capacity. And his egotism is inseparable from his nobility—inseparable, ultimately, from his humanity. This is why Othello "becomes" a representative man: he stands for all men, whose deepest love is tainted with self-regard. The terrible outcome of his story is therefore a commentary on human love in general, a dark mirror of the plight of man, whose love, whose nobility, always contain the seed of their own dissolution.

On both levels of action, the ultimate cause of events is not merely vague or equivocal (as in *Macbeth*); it is unknown, a mystery. This produces on the spectator a profound and extraordinary impression: on the one side a sense of causelessness in human catastrophe, on the other, a sense of its inevitability. We may logically question the ease with which Iago convinces Othello that Desdemona has betrayed him. But on the stage the very speed of transition from faith to doubt creates the illusion of inevitability. Our imaginative experience is such that what is actually sudden conveys an impression of gradualness.

In character as well as in event, causelessness is an insistent note. There is, I think, a truth that Coleridge never intended in his attribution of "motiveless malignity" to Iago. For Iago is, if anything, *over*motivated; he is given so many motives that one is hard put to decide which is the true motive for this or that act. As a result we begin to question the adequacy of all his motives. And, of course, none of his motives is adequate to the monstrosity of his acts.

In Othello, real motive is sicklied o'er by self-righteousness, the ego-flattering delusion that he is acting as an instrument of justice. The murder scene begins with a reprise of the "Othello music" which is even more frigid and marmoreal than before his descent into dissonance.

> It is the cause, it is the cause, my soul.
> Let me not name it to you you chaste stars!
> It is the cause.... (V.ii.1-3)

Othello *thinks* he knows why he will murder his love. But he cannot name the cause; he does not know the cause. He goes on to delude himself further, to build the illusion that he knows what he is doing:

> Put out the light, and then put out the light.
> If I quench thee, thou flaming minister,
> I can again thy former light restore,
> Should I repent me; but once put out thy light,
> Thou cunning'st pattern of excelling nature,
> I know not where is that Promethean heat
> That can thy light relume. (V.ii.7-13)

This cold, logical appraisal is not merely self-justifying; it betrays an astonishing incomprehension of the enormity of what he is about to do. Killing a human person simply cannot be thought of in such terms or expressed in such a style. It is not merely cold; it freezes the heart. The style may deceive us, may keep us from seeing that Othello is ignorant of the real motive of his action, unaware that he is about to destroy (not an object) but an infinitely lovable human person. *Not* the cunning'st pattern of excelling nature, but *Desdemona*.

Neither Othello nor we can name the cause. *It* is the cause. That is to say: *there is no cause*. "Alas the day!" says Desdemona when she sees signs of jealousy in Othello. "I never gave him cause." To which Emilia replies: "But jealous souls will not be answered so./They are not ever jealous for the cause, /But jealous for they are jealous." So, too, at the end, Cassio is mystified. "Dear General," he says to Othello, "I never gave you cause." And when Othello asks why Iago "hath thus ensnared my soul and body," Iago says only: "What you know you know./From this time forth I never will speak word."

This vision of the causeless self-destructiveness of human love and human life (does not Shakespeare anticipate Freud in this?) is what makes *Othello* the most pessimistic of Shakespeare's tragedies. The pathos of Othello's summing up is qualified by a brutal irony. "Then must you speak/Of one that loved not wisely, but too well...." The truth is that he loved neither wisely nor well. The truth is that he never knew how to love at all. The only thing he truly knows is that he "threw a pearl away/ Richer than all his tribe." But he does not know why. And *we* know that he did so, and that many men have done so. But we don't know why.

CHAPTER FIVE

KING LEAR

In the context of this study, *King Lear* is a transitional play. None of the plays so far studied is as direct, as explicit a confrontation of nothingness, none as powerful an exposing of the irrationality of the universe as is *King Lear*. The moral revulsion of *Hamlet* and *Troilus*, the pessimism of *Othello* —these seem to be converted in *Lear* into a kind of *cosmic* nausea. The image of Lear on the heath invoking the gods to destroy the world because his daughters have been unkind to him is an absurd, a nearly farcical image. The cosmic mode of his speeches seems quite incongruous with the domestic, personal feeling that motivates them. One feels, therefore, a strain in the play's rhetoric, as though it were claiming a depth of feeling beyond its structural capacity. Nowhere else in Shakespeare do we find such terrible curses, which are also, as Wilson Knight has noted, very close to bathos and absurdity.

Yet there is also in *Lear* the seed of something that comes to full flower in *Antony and Cleopatra*. I mean a sense of the miracle of human love, an intuition of its transcendence and supreme value. This is expressed primarily in the love between Lear and Cordelia; but it is also expressed in Kent's love, and the Fool's, and Edgar's. This, I think, is what redeems the otherwise terrible vision—"the general curse"—expressed in the play. There is thus in *Lear* the beginning of a "recovery"—the sense that in spite of all evil, human life may be worth living after all. It is as though the creative soul that produced *Hamlet* and *Troilus* and *Othello* had passed through and beyond its "dark night"; as though it were preparing for the creation of *Antony and Cleopatra*, "the Everest of Shakespearian drama," as Wilson Knight has called it. In all this I am, of course, assuming an interpretation of *Lear* which is far from being generally accepted and which I have yet to argue.

In a recent essay John Rosenberg complains of the sentimentalizing that has dominated *Lear* criticism since Bradley.[1] Where Samuel Johnson found unbearable pain, we find "quasi-religious exaltation." A play which is a "pitiless denial of all certainties" has become "a refuge of misplaced piety." But *King Lear*, Rosenberg asserts, "questions everything. It poses for our staggered imaginations the possibility that the cosmos is amoral, perhaps malevolent, more likely a vast nothing. . . ."[2]

I think that Rosenberg is mainly right in these views; but I am thoroughly puzzled by his rejection of Jan Kott's brilliant study of *Lear*:

The play that once seemed to portray salvation through suffering is now misread, in Professor Kott's words, as an image of the decay and fall of the world." Both positions over-simplify a play which is neither a sublime affirmation nor a gross denial, but a savage and beautiful confrontation of the ambiguity of human experience. [3]

One would like to know something more about the ambiguity referred to here; more, too, about the distinction between Rosenberg's view of the play and Kott's. Kott's version of the play *is*, in some sense, an oversimplification and a distortion. There is something in the play that he simply misses, something very hard to define. It is, I think, what Bradley has in mind when he tentatively suggests that there is some sort of qualification of the stark brutality of the play's conclusion.[4] For though Kott comes closer than most critics to the terrible vision at the heart of *Lear*, he yet seems blind to that in the play which transcends Beckettian absurdity, but which can hardly be called Christian (though it is related to both Existentialist and Christian views). In this complex of meaning and feeling, the key terms are life and death, Nothing and love.

The first scene of *Lear* is an obviously expository one: it presents simply and emphatically the initial situation. Yet its clear point has often been blurred under the pressure of piety or habit. Lear, as Freud saw, "is not only an old man; he is a dying man."[5] This is the quite natural motive for his "childish" behavior in the scene. And his insistence that the daughters declare their love in an absurd ritual is but an outward sign of his need for love, a need most importunate in an old man who knows that death will soon take from him everything he holds dear. There is a touch of bathos and self-pity in Lear's avowal that he will "shake all cares and business from our age . . . while we/Unburthened crawl toward death." When a moment later, he "absurdly" demands that his daughters declare their love for him, we ought not to miss the connection between the two passages.

Lear must learn to accept death, says Freud; that, not his need for love, is the essence of his story. Freud sees the three sisters as analogues of the Moerae, who "were created as a result of a recognition which warns man that he too is a part of nature and therefore subject to the immutable law of death."[6] According to Freud, man's imagination struggles against this truth and converts the third of the Sisters from death to love—"the fairest, best, most desirable and the most lovable among women."[7] But this transformation may with equal plausibility mean that love *mitigates* the pang of death, takes away its sting. Freud says of the last scene of Lear that we only need to reverse the situation to see that here the death goddess (Cordelia) is "bearing away the dead hero from the place of battle. . . . Eternal wisdom . . . bids the old man renounce love, choose death and make friends with the necessity of dying."[8] But the final scene has, I believe, a meaning significantly different from this. We shall return to this scene later on.

Aside from conveying Lear's sense of death's nearness and his need for love, the first scene shows us also something of his pride and the ignorance of love's nature that goes with it. He does not understand that love must be freely given and freely accepted. His ignorance of this is precisely the cause of his present desperation. "Nothing will come of nothing," he tells Cordelia; but she knows that love does come of nothing—as Lear will learn through his agony. That she is not simply proud and inflexible here (as a too realistic criticism would have her) is made plain by the text. Her asides during her sisters' protestations—"What shall Cordelia speak? Love and be silent"—these are plainly expository and should not be "psychologized." The most conclusive point of all with respect to Shakespeare's intentions here is the precise meaning of Cordelia's "Nothing" in response to Lear. It is perfectly clear from the context that she does *not* mean that she can and will say nothing about her love—she does in fact say something. She means that she will say nothing "to draw a third more opulent than [her] sisters." In brief: Cordelia refuses to merchandise her love or let Lear do so.

Lear's "Nothing will come of nothing" thus reverberates with ironies. Literally, Cordelia will get nothing if she says nothing. But love *will* come of nothing, and love is not a thing; it transcends the world of things. Lear will come to know his nothingness in the absence of love; and he will come face to face also with the Nothing that is the abyss of death. He will discover also that the orderly nature in which he believes is a delusion—that it, too, is without substance, a form of Nothing. And these discoveries will lead him to an intuition of the transcendent value of love—without which *he* is nothing.

According to John F. Danby, two conceptions of nature engage in dialectical conflict in *King Lear*.[9] As conceived in what Danby calls "Hookerian" terms, nature is an orderly, benign, and God-directed affair, within which reason shows man his proper place and duty. Hobbesian nature, on the other hand, is blind and mechanistic. Man is driven by appetite, and man's reason is primarily a means by which he achieves the ends of appetite. Doubt as to which view of nature is true, says Danby, "pervades the whole of *King Lear* and gives each positive affirmation in the play its peculiar tenseness and clarity."[10] Edmund, Goneril, and Regan represent Hobbesian nature; Lear, Kent, Edgar, and Cordelia represent the traditional Hookerian view. The play, according to Danby explicitly allegorical, balances against each other these conceptions of nature and culminates in the triumph of the Hookerian view, figured in the daughter who "redeems nature in the general curse/Which twain have brought her to."

Danby's "redemptive" reading seems to me wrong-headed on a number of counts—only one of which will be taken up here. His notion that the play is based mainly on two quite distinct views of nature seems to me the most misleading point of all. There can be no question that the play emphatically and repeatedly refers to nature, to different notions of nature, to the disruption of nature, etc. But it is far from clear that the inference to be drawn from this insistence is the one that Danby (and many other critics) draw. Danby's view, I believe, is a product more of wishful piety than of an unbiased study of the text.

There is, of course, nothing ambiguous about Edmund's invocation of (Hobbesian) nature at I.ii.1f., which clearly establishes him as a villain, one of the tribe of Richard Crookback and Iago. And it may be plausibly argued that Lear's invocation of his goddess is addressed to one conceived in Hookerian rather than in Hobbesian terms.

> Hear, Nature, hear! dear goddess, hear!
> Suspend thy purpose, if thou didst intend
> To make this creature fruitful. (I.iv.297-99)

What is not at all apparent is that such a nature really exists. One is reminded of Hotspur's reply to Glendower's brag that he can call spirits from the vasty deep. There is nothing *in the play*, so far as I can see, that supports the view that two natures really exist; on the contrary, everything points to the view that there is only *one* nature, essentially Hobbesian— though we ought to be aware that Shakespeare would hardly have used such terms. To put the matter another way: even assuming that the play describes two divergent ideas of nature as Danby defines them, we might take this to signify their equivalence as plausibly as their opposition. There is in fact much in the play to suggest that equivalence is exactly what is signified.

A little after Edmund's invocation of his goddess, we get a curiously ambiguous speech by Gloucester on the astrological causes of such unnatural events as Kent's banishment and Edgar's presumed perversity.

These late eclipses in the sun and moon portend no good to us.
Though the wisdom of nature can reason it thus and thus, yet
   nature finds itself scourged by the sequent effects. Love cools,
   friendship falls off, brothers divide. In cities, mutinies; in
   countries, discord; in palaces, treason; and the bond cracked
   'twixt son and father. . . .   (I.ii.112-18)

How exactly are we to construe this speech? We see that Gloucester is being duped, that Lear is behaving blindly and stupidly. We might well take the speech as a piece of muddled superstitiousness. Edmund's view that it is an instance of the "admirable evasion of whoremaster man" (glancing at his father's adultery) would then have the force of truth—even though Edmund is clearly a villain.

William R. Elton has convincingly shown that Gloucester's astrological beliefs would be taken by the theologically orthodox as blind superstitiousness; on the other hand, the belief in astrology, Elton admits, pervaded Elizabethan society.[11] We have also to reckon with the fact that the speech occurs in the context of an emphatically pre-Christian play, and with Shakespeare's tendency to make soothsaying and astrological influence dramatically credible.

All of which brings us back to the immediate dramatic situation in which the speech occurs. Since we see how, in this situation, Gloucester plays the fool, his speech has the force of an "admirable evasion" indeed. And since Gloucester is appealing (whatever the distortion) to an order, an aspect of cosmic order, of the sort envisaged by the Hookerian idea of nature, the passage has the effect of calling into question the very existence of such a nature, and of rendering belief in it absurd.

A similar effect, intensified by multiple ironies, is produced by Gloucester's calling Edmund a "loyal and natural boy" (glancing again at his adultery, at Edmund's bastardy, and *blurring* the distinction between the two natures). Gloucester urges Edmund to avenge his blinding, to "enkindle all the sparks of nature/To quit this horrid act" (III.vii.86-87), once again appealing to a "nature" (Edmund's) in which he is utterly deceived and to the (Hookerian) nature in which he is a fool to believe.

When Kent hears of Cordelia's goodness, he remarks:

> It is the stars,
> The stars above us, govern our conditions,
> Else one self mate and mate could not beget
> Such different issues. (IV.iii.34-37)

Kent is one of the "good" characters in the play, and, presumably, a believer in Hookerian nature. Yet this speech clearly echoes Gloucester's "late eclipses" speech—even while its intention (Kent's) is to *deny* rationality to the human and natural order. And if we put the two speeches together, as I think we should, what emerges is a vision of blind and confused morals snatching at pious and empty catch-phrases in order to bring some meaning into a world which has utterly lost it. Edgar's counsel to his father—

> Think that the clearest gods, who make them honors
> Of men's impossibilities, have preserved thee— (IV.vi.73-74)

is a lie. It is Edgar's love and his trickery that have preserved Gloucester, not the gods.

If we now look back at the first scene, we may, I think, see the dramatic point of Cordelia's apparent coldness in telling Lear that she loves him "according to my bond, no more nor less." She sees that his attempt to deal with love in terms of the traditional, rational order is absurd. And so she replies with strict rationality. Those critics are right who regard her speeches at this point as embodying a traditional Hookerian view of the relations between father and child. But what they miss is the irony: Cordelia is pointing out the inadequacy of this view in dealing with love. In a way, she is reducing that view to absurdity.

This is precisely the burden of Lear's first great insight in the play. When Regan points out how irrational is Lear's need of attendants ("What need one?"), he replies:

> O, reason not the need! Our basest beggars
> Are in the poorest thing superfluous.
> Allow not nature more than nature needs,
> Man's life is cheap as beast's. (II.iv.267-70)

Lear sees for the first time that there is a dimension to man which nature, however conceived, cannot comprehend. (The emphasis in the first line of the passage quoted should go on *reason*, not on *need*.) This is the beginning of wisdom for Lear, the wisdom that culminates in his mad vision of unaccommodated man as a poor, bare, forked animal, and of his own contingency and mortality—

> They told me I was everything, 'Tis a lie—I am
> not ague-proof. (IV.vi.106-7)

The view of nature which finally emerges in the play is brutally pointed by Albany's "The gods defend her!" a moment before Lear enters with Cordelia dead in his arms. What we see and feel ("She's gone forever!") is hardly in accord with either Danby's piety or Edgar's

> The gods are just, and of our pleasant vices
> Make instruments to scourge us. (V.iii.170-71)

(which ironically echoes Regan's "pious" speech at II.iv.305-7).

The gods are neither just nor unjust; they do not exist. So far as nature in the play is definable at all, it is the nature that Edmund worships, a nature essentially Hobbesian, which destroys indifferently her worshippers and nonworshippers. In such a world only human love can make life endurable; for human love transcends the world of nature.

The ordinary reader's view that *Lear* is a play about filial ingratitude is not far off the mark—though it needs careful qualification. There is a tremendous weight of feeling in Lear's sense of outrage at the treatment he receives at his daughters' hands. This is based upon his implicit belief in a just natural order which imposes on child and parent unbreachable duties. Lear is blind to the parental side of this order. But he is also blind (and this is his crucial blindness) to the absence of any sanction or ground in objective reality for this belief. Goneril and Regan show him the true status of child-parent relations conceived of rationally and this truth drives him toward madness.

It is only in his madness, and in his passage through it, that Lear recognizes and accepts his own nothingness; in the poverty of spirit which he then momentarily achieves, he sees that only love can redeem the world of nature. Both Lear and Gloucester throw off in the course of the play "artificial" identities which have been based on erroneous belief. Lear learns that he is but a man, that he has been flattered like a dog. And it is right that such insight should come to him through violent contact with physical (Hobbesian) nature (the heath, the storm, flowers). It is precisely the vision of Hobbesian nature which points to the need for the love which transcends it and makes its cruelty bearable. That, I think, is what Shakespeare meant us to see in *Lear*. It is not a vision which appeals to conventional piety.

Danby's treatment of the Fool is, I think, the best thing in his book; yet he gets the Fool's tone slightly askew. The Fool, he says, is "the consciousness of a split society," torn apart by the antagonism of head and heart. The Fool's

head thinks with the Reason of Goneril and Regan, yet what he does is directly counter to the self-interest which for them and for him is the only thing that makes sense. His greatest bit of cruelty is wrung from him by compassion. While he counsels flight, with wiseman and knave, he will not desert the king: because he is a Fool. What he does will not square with what he says, and it is a redeeming insincerity. Wilfully and blindly he holds to the Great Wheel going downhill.[12]

This account seems logically correct, yet it completely misses the Fool's peculiar irony. Persistently, and with bitter, self-mocking irony, the Fool describes attitudes he clearly contemns. He does not, as Danby suggests, accept these attitudes intellectually. There is no conflict between head and heart in the Fool—as there is, say, in Enobarbus. He simply speaks ironically:

> All that follow their noses are led by their eyes but blind men, and
> there's not a nose among twenty but can smell him that's stinking.
> Let go thy hold when a great wheel runs down a hill, lest it break
> thy neck with following it; but the great one that goes upward,
> let him draw thee after. When a wise man gives thee better counsel,
> give me mine again. I would have none but knaves follow it, since
> a fool gives it. (II.iv.69-78)

Here, as almost always, the Fool is teaching his hearers the way of the world. He speaks bitterly—not, perhaps, as bitterly as Thersites or Apemantus—and his bitterness comes from direct knowledge of the world and his belief that it should not be as it is. Not for a moment is he tempted by the worldly wisdom of the "politician." He has only profound contempt for the "wise" followers of ego-centered reason. All this is eloquently expressed in his playing on the paradoxes of wisemen and fools. It is certified by the little song which concludes the speech just quoted.

> That sir which serves and seeks for gain,
>   And follows but for form,
> Will pack when it begins to rain
>   And leave thee in the storm.
> But I will tarry; the fool will stay,
>   And let the wise man fly.

> The knave turns fool that runs away;
> The fool no knave, perdy. (II.iv.79-86)

The knave turns fool that runs away, and the fool will stay: that is, staying is truly wisdom, and the worldly wiseman that flies is the true fool. The truth of this is demonstrated in the play by both Kent and Edgar, both of whom are rejected by, yet serve to the end, those they love. The Fool speaks his wisdom out of his own pain and it can therefore never be shaken. "The head," says Danby, "would betray [the Fool] back to Goneril's hearth. . . . But for reasons neither he nor the head knows he follows Lear over the heath."[13] But the Fool *knows* why he follows Lear: he loves the old man, and he is no knave.

The issue, I think, hinges on the matter of tone. Wilson Knight remarks, acutely:

The core of the play is an absurdity, an indignity, an incongruity. In no tragedy of Shakespeare does incident and dialogue so recklessly and miraculously walk the tight-rope of our pity over the depths of bathos and absurdity.[14]

This comes very close to the ingredients of the Fool's tone. It is not quite the tone of Beckett; it is not the emotional concomitant of perceiving existential absurdity. This is why Kott's reading of the play misses the mark—though it comes closer to a true reading than Danby's. The trouble with Kott's view is that it is too *purely* Beckettian and therefore misses the precise incongruity that Knight remarks: Shakespeare's *own* incongruity. In the *Lear* world there is love: its existence, especially when seen in the brutal context of Hobbesian nature, is at once a miracle and an absurdity. Love does not, so far as I can tell, inhabit Beckett's world, and that, I think, accounts for the difference in tone between Beckett and Lear's Fool. A proper reading of *Lear* should neglect neither its brutal "naturalism" nor the human love which transcends it. This transcending love does not "redeem Nature," for it is not part of nature. But it redeems human life.

There are two truths that Lear comes finally to grasp in the course of his agony. He learns not to pray to the gods—the keepers of Hookerian nature—because he discovers that the gods are not there. And if Nothing is there, then his belief that he deserves love is a delusion. This is the delusion that motivates his demand for declarations of love by his daughters at the beginning of the play. It is founded on a prior belief in rationality and order in nature. But if Nothing is there, reason and order have lost their divine sanction, and love can no longer be assumed as an inherent bond in that order. Thus, there may be a fine and deliberate irony in Cordelia's telling Lear that she loves him "according to my bond, no more nor less." Cordelia may or may not believe in the traditional order; but she perceives clearly that the world of love transcends it. Thus her "Nothing" in response to Lear's question has even richer overtones than we first thought.

Lear comes to understand and to feel this in his own flesh when he cries:

> O, reason not the need! Our basest beggars
> Are in the poorest thing superfluous.
> Allow not nature more than nature needs,
> Man's life is cheap as beast's (II.ii.267-70)

Only inveterate and blinding piety could turn this into a "redemptive" text. The nature referred to here is clearly *not* Hookerian. Reason is an instrument of policy, not of love. And in the order of nature, where love is absent, man's status is indistinguishable from that of animals. Lear puts the case even more succinctly when, in his madness, he perceives that "unaccommodated man" is but "a poor, bare, forked animal." Only outside of nature is there relief for pain, only, that is, in love. Lear comes to see this through suffering and under the constant imminence of death—which is but another name for Nothing.[15] The full realization of these truths comes to Lear only in the full tide of his madness; this is the "reason in madness" that constitutes the ultimate paradox of the play's pervasive paradoxicality. This "rational" contradictoriness is imaged in the grotesque heath scenes (especially II.ii and III.vi), where mad Lear, and "mad" Edgar, blind Gloucester, and the Fool come together. The intensity of feeling here seems to overpower the very means of expression, so that one is not sure whether or not the play has fallen into bathos.

These are Lear's first sane words on seeing Cordelia:

> You do me wrong to take me out o' the' grave.
> Thou art a soul in bliss; but I am bound
> Upon a wheel of fire, that mine own tears
> Do scald like molten lead.   (IV.iv.45-48)

His pain is now the pain of contrition and love; he is aware, for the first time in his life, of Cordelia's infinite worth and of his own unworthiness. He has come to this awareness by passing through and beyond a vision of Nothing (his own and the world's) to a sense of transcendence. Nothing is there, but what has truly been and truly *is*, is a moment of human love in the darkness: one self has given itself and recognized another, and that makes all the difference. "If you have poison for me," he says, "I will drink it." He thus sums up his willingness now to die—and this constitutes his transformation after his passage through madness. When he realizes his situation, he says to Cordelia: "I know you do not love me . . . .You have some cause. . . ." And she instructs him: "No cause, no cause." She is teaching him about the world of love which transcends the world of causes.

And in the last scene, when he and Cordelia are being led off to prison, he seems to have learned the most important lesson of his life. He sees that life and death are themselves of no real consequence, for he loves and is beloved.

> Come, let's away to prison.
> We two alone will sing like birds i' th' cage.
> When thou dost ask me blessing, I'll kneel down
> And ask of thee forgiveness. So we'll live,
> And pray, and sing, and tell old tales, and laugh
> At gilded butterflies, and hear poor rogues
> Talk of Court news; and we'll talk with them too—
> Who loses and who wins; who's in, who's out—
> And take upon 's the mystery of things,
> As if we were God's spies; and we'll wear out,
> In a walled prison, packs and sects of great ones
> That ebb and flow by the moon.   (V.iii.8-19)

This is the insight contained, in a different tone, in the Fool's songs about wisemen and fools and the way of the world. Pain and madness have taught Lear the meaning of love; he now possesses the wisdom which is foolishness in the world's eyes. That is why he can now take upon him the mystery of things and laugh at gilded butterflies.

Yet when Cordelia is taken from him, he does not remain in this state; he regresses to the rage and mad protest of earlier scenes. He cannot accept *her* death, and the agony of his loss has seemed too much for even a Samuel Johnson to bear. There is something unexpected in the final scene: just when Lear seems to have reached a kind of serenity and acceptance, we are suddenly plunged back into the worst, most painful moment of the play. Yet Cordelia *must* die: we can sense this if we set against Shakespeare's play the happy ending of the source story or of Tate's version. Cordelia must die, but it is not easy to explain why. The much mooted question as to whether Lear thinks Cordelia alive or dead at the end is really beside the point. In either case, the cruelty of the scene is unrelieved. Why must Cordelia die?

In terms of theme, the question approaches its own answer. In the reconciliation scene (so we have argued) Lear has reached a degree of insight and humility; his insight (which we are meant to share) includes the awareness that all *things* are ultimately without value, but that a beloved person has infinite value. Thus, life and death are of no consequence, because love, which might be called an intuition of the value of persons, transcends both life and death. Yet Lear, imperfect in love and knowledge at the end of the play, has not fully grasped this—and no wonder, since he is a weak and dying old man. But *we* are not meant to share his agony: that is the *dramatic* paradox of the final scene.

Lear's "Never, never, never, never, never" brings home to *us* the absoluteness of love's transcendence even while it expresses Lear's desolation. Lear sees and suffers the absurdity of Cordelia's death. And *we* perceive that to *be* Cordelia (and for Cordelia to be) is in some indefinable way a supreme and transcendent good. Lear experiences this truth—it is inseparable from his agony. And in that final image of Lear with his beloved dead in his arms, *we* are enabled to see the worst cruelty the world can inflict *and* the love which transcends that cruelty. To put it differently: Cordelia's death signifies at once the world's absurdity and the ultimate inconsequence of death. Cordelia cannot ever not be. That is why Cordelia's death is the play's only possible ending.

Lear's story involves his entry into the world of impersonal Nature and his discovery that, though a king, he smells of mortality. And he concurrently learns the meaning of love. These truths are expressed by Cordelia's death as emphatically as may be. No other ending would have the same rightness and power. This is not, to be sure, a Christian vision; but neither is it the Beckettian one that Kott describes so eloquently. Lear's heartbreak, says Maynard Mack, "is precisely the measure of what in our world of relatedness, it is possible to lose and possible to win. The victory and the defeat are simultaneous and inseparable."[16]

CHAPTER SIX

RECAPITULATION

Looking back over the works we have studied, we may discern certain recurrences of attitude and of thematic emphasis. There is nothing very precise about this pattern; even to call it a pattern is to suggest something more deliberate than what I have in mind. There is simply a kind of "progress" or development that emerges in the sequence of these works which is undeniable but which is very difficult to formulate because the elements that recur are themselves continually changing their outward form. That is why I am using terms more inclusive and vague than would ordinarily be desirable in literary analysis.

In the earlier historical tetralogy, there is an intense fascination with political power, with men's lust for it, and with the problems—social, political, and moral—which are raised by its pursuit and possession and loss. The saintly, politically inept King Henry VI is contrasted with the bloody-minded Duke of York and his sons—constrasted indeed with all those driven by power-lust or vengeance, who will stop at nothing to attain their ends. In *Richard III* we get in Richard Crookback the climax of the fascinated horror with which the machiavel is regarded throughout these plays. Richard focuses in his person a profound ambivalence: revulsion and awe, terror and irrepressible admiration. Though the means to his ascendancy are horrifying, he brings order of a sort to a nation that is disintegrating socially and politically—the order that Henry could never bring.

The vision expressed in these plays is indeed, as Kott points out, a nightmare; the Grand Mechanism is an eternal and horrible force, operating in history much like an Aeschylean curse. But there is also present a sense of England's need, the yearning for order and an end to the spilling of blood. What sort of king can bring England order and peace?

This question is answered, ambiguously, in the Lancastrian tetralogy. Richard II is unquestionably a bad king; far from bringing order to England, he brings chaos, he destroys the very order by which he rules. Yet Richard remains God's anointed deputy, and it is treason, it is sacrilegious to depose him. So, in the play, as soon as we are certain that Richard will fall, our sympathies shift from Bolingbroke to him. Bolingbroke, who has been unjustly treated by the king, comes to claim his own and set things right in England. Yet when it becomes clear (and there is a remarkable ambiguity about this matter in the play) that Bolingbroke means to depose his lawful sovereign, the spectator is faced with an irresolvable dilemma. It is a dilemma, at any rate, which Shakespeare does not resolve in the rest of the tetralogy.

The ambivalence of the earlier tetralogy is present, in a different, more sophisticated form throughout the Henry plays. In his adroit manipulation of men and moments, Bolingbroke is a more sophisticated Richard III. He is not regarded with horror, but with a kind of grudging admiration. His political adroitness, his urbane machiavellianism, if you will, is nonetheless seen as inseparable from his suppression of human feeling and tenderness. They love not poison that do poison need, says Bolingbroke. And the sadness of that sentence is Shakespeare's as well as Bolingbroke's.

On the other side, the human, the infinitely various personal side of human being is embodied in Falstaff and Hotspur and Richard II. There is profound sympathy and admiration for all of them; but there is also an unblinking realization of the social destructiveness of each of them. Falstaff and the anarchic impulses he embodies must be checked if society is to survive. So too with the politically destructive Hotspur—whose virtues are inseparable from his destructiveness—and with the egoistic Richard.

Behind the facade of the ideal king, even Prince Hal shows himself a machiavel, a not unworthy son of Bolingbroke—which is what, of course, he always wants to be. That he is a somewhat more attractive figure than his father may be attributed to Shakespeare's having recognized the necessities of politics and the limitations of human personality. Political order demands strong rulers like Bolingbroke and Hal; but such rulers must abandon something of their own humanity. Falstaff must needs be cast off; Hotspur must be destroyed. Shakespeare seems to perceive that kingship is no longer either divinely sanctioned or viable in terms of the traditional moral order—and in this he speaks for his age. Political order and national survival in the seventeenth century will require the rule of a single-minded, machiavellian king, unfettered by moral or religious scruples, unaffected by human emotions.

In the history plays, then, there is an emphatic opposition between "political" virtues, the masculine rationality and self-control that make for worldly success, and the personal values connected with human feeling, with beauty, with love. These values, these human potentialities, appear in the histories to be mutually exclusive and irreconcilable. It is just this perception, and especially its consequences for Shakespeare's vision of human life, that leads him into the moral issues at the heart of the tragedies which follow in the next decade.

In *Julius Caesar* (1599), a morally good, a "principled" protagonist heroically represses his love for Caesar for what he believes to be a political good. We watch in horror as the noble and well-intentioned Brutus helps to bring about—not merely political chaos—but his own spiritual destruction and dishonor. Nothing could more potently express a revulsion at political ideals and the self-delusion to which they lead than the consequences of Brutus' decision to join the conspirators. Rome is not better but worse for Caesar's murder; the only one who does not see that clearly is Brutus himself. And in the bitter irony that inheres in his story we may read a partial resolution of the ambivalence of the history plays. Political values are devalued, personal ones are elevated; yet the two kinds of value are still seen as irreconcilable. Their irreconcilability indeed might be regarded as the key to this particular play.

Hamlet's philosophical skepticism and sexual revulsion express his profound despair, his abandonment of belief in the traditional order by which he (and sixteenth century Englishmen) lived. That is precisely the cause of the sense of frustrated action that pervades the play. The disease that afflicts Hamlet is endemic in *Troilus and Cressida*, where we get an image of a world utterly without meaning and order. In *Troilus* Hamlet's vision is actualized, staggering the imagination. All the possibilities of response to such a world are figured in the chief characters of the play—and we are given to see that they are all inadequate. In *Julius Caesar, Hamlet,* and *Troilus* the love theme—the emotional and intuitive side of human life—figures importantly. It is a bitterly betrayed value in *Julius Caesar.* In *Hamlet* love itself is contaminated by the general skepticism that afflicts Hamlet and takes the form of misogyny and sexual disgust. In *Troilus* this skepticism and disgust is amplified and intensified; love is reduced to lust, is enslaved by time. The impossibility of love is in a way the symbol of a world without value or meaning. So Troilus' absurd refusal to believe his eyes when he sees Cressida betray him is closely related to Hamlet's brutal treatment of Ophelia in the nunnery scene; and Troilus' "What is aught but as 'tis valued" is closely related to Hamlet's "There's nothing either good or bad but thinking makes it so."

In *Othello* a classically shaped and nearly perfect form tends to mask a substance of profound pessimism. It is the story of true love in which love and goodness serve only to bring about their own destruction—do so with an awful inevitability. We see that true love is doomed because of its unavoidable dependence on self-love. The lovers are enmeshed in a net fashioned of their own goodness—that is the basis for the profound horror in the play. The generalized pessimism of *Hamlet* and *Troilus* is here focused on *human* nature.

Despite the magniloquence of its invocation of chaos (a reprise of the meaninglessness of the *Troilus* world), *Lear* is most remarkable for its glimpses of hope after so much despair. For in the midst of pain and darkness, cruelty and madness, there shines the figure of Cordelia and the love she bestows upon the pain-wracked Lear. It is Lear's recognition of the Nothing that engulfs him, of the nothingness of his own momentary being, that teaches him the absolute sole value of love. This new vision of human life which begins to emerge in *Lear* comes to full expression in *Antony and Cleopatra*. It is, indeed only in the light of the total development that we have here sketched that we can see clearly the full meaning of that rather mystical play. The seeds of this meaning, hints of what is to come, can be found in the Sonnets a decade or more earlier. In the opposition between the platonic love of the Fair Youth series and the sexual disgust of the Dark Woman series, we may see the condition which demands resolution and finds it in *Antony and Cleopatra*—where flesh and spirit are reconciled in the love between a man and a woman.

CHAPTER SEVEN

ANTONY AND CLEOPATRA

Both the form and the meaning of *Antony and Cleopatra* are upsetting—radically different from Shakespeare's earlier tragedies. One's initial response to the play, therefore, is a tendency to reduce it to familiar categories and so make it "manageable," to see it as a kind of cautionary exemplum in which a noble but flawed hero kisses away kingdoms and is finally destroyed by his slavery to passion.[1] The ordinary man of Shakespeare's time would have understood Antony's story in that way; on the basis of such hard evidence, Shakespeare is often equated with the least common denominator of the time.

Professor Wimsatt is a notable exception. He recognizes the play's greatness, but he considers it immoral:

> By any ethical standard at all what Antony does to Fulvia, to Octavia especially, to his political allegiance, to himself, to Cleopatra even, must be bad. Yet the death of Antony and of Cleopatra is in the high Roman fashion, what's brave, what's noble.... We are called upon to admire Antony and Cleopatra. In short, the play is immoral.[2]

But the issue of the play's morality is a false issue, one that arises, in part, as a consequence of its radical newness. As sometimes happens with a great artist, Shakespeare transcended in *Antony and Cleopatra* the tragic form which he partly inherited and partly helped to perfect. He created a radically new form expressive of a vision which the older form could not express.[3]

As the play begins, an almost anonymous Roman tells us that we shall see in Antony "The triple pillar of the world transformed/Into a strumpet's fool." A moment later, that is just what we do see:

> *Cleo.* If it be love indeed, tell me how much.
> *Ant.* There's beggary in the love that can be reckoned.
> *Cleo.* I'll set a bourn how far to be beloved.
> *Ant.* Then must thou needs find out new heaven, new earth.
> (I.i.14-17)

Their speech seems to mock itself with its own affectation; it is the language not of lovers, but of parodists of love. There is irony in the conceits, for they will later assume real validity. But now they sound worn out, formulary, conveying both the meretriciousness of their relationship and their awareness that it is so. They are playing a tawdry game, whose rules and risks they both know, whose stakes are pleasant and desirable—but no great matter.

The initial "Roman" estimate of the lovers is thus confirmed out of their own mouths. Yet before their play is done, they will address each other in language which will give this initial estimate the lie. Even now Antony uses imagery which will in the end be just and true:

> Let Rome in Tiber melt . . .
> Kingdoms are clay; our dungy earth alike
> Feeds beast as man. (I.i.33-36)

"Excellent falsehood," says Cleopatra. Antony, of course, knows that it is. So he tells her to quit chiding and wasting time: "There's not a minute of our lives should stretch/Without some pleasure now." Pleasure: that is the present keynote. It is made to seem as attractive as it really is, and both of them know exactly what it is worth.

We are therefore not surprised to see how easily, in the next scene, Antony can shake off his Egyptian fetters. His exploitation of Cleopatra and his imperial ambitions do not fundamentally conflict with each other; both stem from the egotistic drive toward possession and dominance.[4] When Antony's political status is threatened, he therefore scarcely hesitates; leaving Cleopatra gives him as little pain as did the loss of Fulvia. Enobarbus, whose supervenient irony always implies other viewpoints than the one he states, puts the case precisely. "Under a compelling occasion let women die. It were a pity to cast them away for nothing, though, between them and a great cause they should be esteemed nothing."

The Antony we first know in the play is thus essentially egotistic; yet there are signs that he possesses potentialities of a different sort. His attraction to Cleopatra, who stands for all that is beyond the practical and rational in human life, is in itself suggestive. And when Enobarbus comments on Cleopatra's celerity in dying, Antony replies like one bemused: "She is cunning past man's thought." He is befuddled by his inability to reduce to the categories of masculine reason the infinite variety, the instinctive life, of which she is so dazzling an embodiment. And he is fascinated, too.

It is Cleopatra who comes close to loving in these early scenes. Her attachment seems at first as superficial as Antony's. But this impression soon gives way to another: that she is simply not aware of the depth of her involvement. She knows the nature of Antony's passion; but she wants the pretense anyway: "Good now, play one scene/Of excellent dissembling, and let it look/Like perfect honour." And her continual chiding—does it not signify her fear of losing him, her anxiety at the fragility of her hold? "Cross him in nothing," Charmian advises. "Thou teachest like a fool," she replies, "the way to lose him." Cleopatra is no doubt in the right, for she knows her lover with cunning past man's thought.

And then when *she* takes leave of *him*, it is as though her own passion surprises her. She speaks as one who has lost the right words for the game—because the game has suddenly become serious:

> Sir, you and I must part—but that's not it.
> Sir, you and I have loved—but there's not it.
> That you know well. Something it is I would—
> O, my oblivion is a very Antony,
> And I am all forgotten!   (I.iii.87-91)

She really *is* distracted: even while she ridicules Antony's formulary goodbyes, even while she mocks at her own situation, love has taken her unawares. In these early scenes, then, we begin to see that she is capable of a love different from the loves of her salad days, a love so strange to her that it will come to full realization only through intense suffering.

Her suffering is dramatized in those wonderful messenger scenes (II.v; II.iii) where our sympathy does not go out to the messenger (who deserves it) but to her. The first of these scenes opens in an atmosphere of sensual brightness. The badinage is charged with sexual overtones, which suggest, not dark passion, but a mature cognizance of the delight that lives in the sensual nature, a ripened joy in that part of man which even the theologian holds to be good in itself. "Ram thou thy fruitful tidings in mine ears," Cleopatra tells the messenger, "That long time have been barren." But then she hardly gives him a chance to speak, for she sees no goodness in his face.

A moment later, when he tells her that Antony is married, she cries, "The most infectious pestilence upon thee!" and beats him mercilessly. She insists on hearing the terrible news again and again, each time raging at the news bearer—until, finally, the poor fellow flees for his life. By the end of the scene we know her capacity for suffering and depth of her love. And so does she:

> Let him forever go!—let him not!—Charmian,
> Though he be painted one way like a Gorgon,
> The other way's a Mars.—Bid you Alexas
> Bring me word how tall she is.—Pity me, Charmian,
> But do not speak to me. Lead me to my chamber.
>
> (II.v.115-19)

In the companion scene (III.iii) she is a chastened and wiser woman, managing a precarious balance this side of despair by believing the half-truths of the messenger—who has also become wiser.

It is not so much the *quality* of Cleopatra's love that changes in the course of the play (it changes much less than Antony's) as it is the extent of her self-awareness. It is natural that she should so little understand herself, for it is the other principle—masculine and rational—which makes for understanding. Yet, while the overplus of the instinctive and irrational remains throughout, it is touched toward the end by the masculine, so that she becomes ever so slightly more "Roman." After Antony dies, it is as though a vestige of him survives in her, steadying and ennobling her, and quickening her perceptions.

Antony also undergoes a period of suffering, but before it begins, our vision of the play's fictive world changes. In the first act, the Roman estimate of Antony and his relation to Cleopatra is a valid one: seen through Roman eyes, Antony does indeed approve the common liar at Rome, and Roman values are supreme. But even before the relation between the lovers begins to alter, these values depreciate; and they become less and less worthy as the love between the protagonists rises in value—until finally Roman values seem nearly worthless and Caesar himself is an "ass unpolicied."

This process begins as early as II.ii, where Antony appears as "politic" with Caesar as he was, a little earlier, with Cleopatra. Inventing transparent alibis for clear faults, pursuing "policy" with offhand skill, he is sympathetic only by contrast with Caesar, who strikes one as a bloodless, not quite human creature. They are all engaged in the quest for power, a game that enforces lies and temporizing—and the appearance of honor.

Enobarbus tells the true nature of this game when he speaks his honest soldier's truth (II.ii.102-5). And though he is rebuked by Antony, he has the final word: "That truth should be silent I had almost forgot." In the same scene, after Caesar has *used* Octavia to patch his differences with Antony and so enhance his power, Enobarbus gives his celebrated description of Cleopatra in her barge. The splendor of the description, keeping before our mind's eye the queen who beggars all description (and who has her own kind of integrity and truth), puts the preceding politicking in a bad light indeed.

This downgrading of Roman values continues in the scene aboard Pompey's galley (II.vii), for which Plutarch provided scant raw material, and which therefore deserves careful scrutiny. The pillars of the world (Caesar excepted) abandon themselves to Bacchus and so show themselves to be merely mortal, subject to chance and change. "The least wind in the world," says a servant, "will blow them down." And in vino veritas. When Menas offers Pompey the world if he will let him cut the cable, Pompey refuses. Menas, he says, should have cut the cable without telling him. For "'Tis not my profit that does lead mine honor;/Mine honor, it." Such is the nature of Roman honor, and such the radical contingency of power.

In the same scene there is more sense than may at first glance appear in Antony's inane description of Egyptian reptiles. Apart from the palpable allusion to Antony's serpent of old Nile, we may discern here the emergence of a complex symbol which will burgeon with meaning as the play moves to its end. "Your serpent of Egypt," says Lepidus, "is bred now of your mud by the operation of your sun." It is a strange serpent indeed, shaped like itself, living by what nourishes it. Irreducible to rational categories, it is a rich symbol of the dung of human life out of which the noblest life may emerge—as the noblest love may emerge out of sexual passion. It is an immortal worm, too, for, the "elements once out of it, it transmigrates." We will meet it again.

If we take the series of battle scenes in acts III and IV to be depicting the stages of Antony's defeat, they seem oddly redundant. Shakespeare draws out the process of his defeat, I think, so that he may articulate the progress of inner change in him—which *takes* time, takes, in any case, dramatic time.

We are never really in much doubt as to who will win the worldly struggle. The Soothsayer early on prophesied that Charmian had "seen and proved a fairer former fortune/Than that which is to approach." And at Rome he told Antony to put space between himself and Caesar, for "If thou dost play with him at any game,/Thou art sure to lose." Caesar is suited to the world and naturally dominates it. Antony's demon is "noble, courageous, high, unmatchable,/Where Caesar's is not. But near him thy angel/Becomes a fear, as being o'erpowered." After the pleas of Enobarbus and Canidius, moreover, we are virtually certain that Antony's decision to fight by sea is a fatal one. We have seen Pompey laugh away his fortune, and we have Enobarbus' word for it that "he cannot weep 't back again."

The worldly game, then, is up for Antony almost before it begins. But at this point in the play, that is not what chiefly concerns us, for Roman empire has by now lost a good deal of its savor. We are concerned rather with Antony's relation to Cleopatra, a relation intensified and complicated by the suffering which the outward events have engendered. Even before his first defeat, the rational, egotistic tendency in Antony has begun to give way to a different element in his nature. We see this in his allowing Cleopatra to take part in the war and in his decision to fight by sea. As Enobarbus puts it, "A diminution in our Captain's brain/Restores his heart." That fairly epitomizes the process we are about to witness: Antony is becoming less soldierly, less masculine, less rational—and more truly a lover. Our attitude to this change is, of course, quite different from Enobarbus'.

Antony's suffering begins with his first defeat. He is overcome with shame at having fled the battle, pursuing Cleopatra "like a doting mallard" (surely a symbolic incident). "I have fled myself," he says. Indeed: he is not the same as he was. His defeat brings home to him for the first time the sacrifice of self he must make for another person. It is not easy for him. Such an uprooting and realignment of the personality at its deepest levels causes intense pain. Antony suffers, as it were, a loss of selfhood; this not only issues in deep psychic pain, but makes possible further change, fresh perception, and more pain. That is why he shows such astonishing reversals of attitude and feeling throughout these scenes—even as he moves all the while toward acceptance of his love and a recognition of its supreme value as opposed to the value of the world he gives up.

He does not quite realize the personal meaning or the finality of his first defeat; he is perhaps too "unqualitied with very shame." So he blames his defeat on Cleopatra's fearful sails. But we can discern that he is really speaking of his (for him quite strange) subjection to love: "O, whither has thou led me, Egypt?" She begs forgiveness: "I little thought/You would have followed." But that is a momentary lie. She wanted him to follow, without perhaps being fully aware of it. It is her way of keeping him from the world's great snare. And Antony very nearly perceives this:

> Egypt, thou knew'st too well
> My heart was to thy rudder tied by th' strings,
> And thou shouldst tow me after. O'er my spirit

> Thy full supremacy thou knew'st, and that
> Thy beck might from the bidding of the gods
> Command me.   (III.xi.56-61)

She does not deny it, she merely pleads for pardon. And since Antony has not yet realized the absoluteness of his bondage or his loss, he comes round with relative ease. "Fall not a tear, I say. One of them rates/All that is won and lost." When full realization comes to him in the following scenes, he will not find it so easy to forgive her.

His next access of anger and anguish occurs in the Thyreus scene (III.xiii), where it is wrong to assume that Cleopatra intends to betray him. She is only being her irrational self. Antony's virulent outburst here seems therefore excessive. He veers to the point of view of self-regarding reason and, with Roman eyes, see the dearest image of love's eyes transformed into a monster:

> You were half blasted ere I knew you. Ha!
> Have I my pillow left unpressed in Rome,
> Forborne the getting of a lawful race,
> And by a gem of women, to be abused
> By one that looks on feeders?   (III.xiii.105-9)

He is, of course, unfair. But so speaks the rational self, reacting against the instinctive one which has deprived it of power and freedom. It will speak again, but never again with quite such vehemence. Henceforth, in spite of temporary reversions, Antony will move steadily toward acceptance, toward an intuition of the rightness of his destiny. Now, after having Thyreus whipped (an act very like Cleopatra's irrational treatment of the messenger), and after Cleopatra has protested her love, his rage subsides. A diminution of the captain's brain is restoring his heart, and, as Cleopatra knows, she "must stay his time."

Beginning with the second scene of act IV, a new mood gradually pervades the play, one which will grow more intense as the play moves to its end. This mood first takes the form of sad, resigned expectancy. We see Antony giving up—in a kind of formal renunciation—the military-political grandeur to which he has devoted his life. He calls forth his loyal servants, clasps their hands, and in effect bids them farewell. Cleopatra is mystified: there is something here she does not understand. "What means this?" she asks Enobarbus, who (though he understands well enough) replies with his inveterate irony: "'Tis one of those old tricks which sorrow shoots/Out of the mind." The sense of impending doom becomes almost palpable;

Antony's rhetorical flair becomes a simple and natural eloquence. "Well, my fellows, wait on me tonight. . . ." Again Cleopatra demands an explanation of Enobarbus and is again put off by his irony—though a moment later even he is "onion eyed." Enobarbus knows that nothing will make her understand why Antony and his followers are grieving. And our awareness that she will never understand this side of Antony intensifies the scene's sadness, for we perceive therein the ultimate, impassable limit of human love.

Toward the end of the scene, Antony becomes explicit:

> I look on you
> As one who takes his leave. Mine honest friends,
> I turn you not away; but like a master
> Married to your good service, stay till death. (IV.ii.28-31)

Death is in the offing now, and its constant nearness helps to sustain the mood which will shortly supersede this sad one. It is a dreamlike ambience, a shadowy sense of the private world of lovers who live in a sort of "separated" state, a world sealed off from the world of physical reality. Even before this, Antony and Cleopatra have begun to address each other in the private accents of lovers from whom all pretense has been purged away. They have begun, in short, to address each other as persons: "O my lord, my lord. . . ." "Love, I am full of lead." "Ah, dear, if I be so. . . ." Now (in IV.iv) they really seem to be living in a world they have made for each other.

> *Ant.*   Eros! mine armor, Eros!
> *Cleo.*   Sleep a little.
> *Ant.*   No, my chuck. Eros, come . . .
> *Cleo.*   Nay, I'll help too. (IV.iv.1-5)

Antony now goes to battle, not to gain the world for himself, but as a husband, to win trophies for his love: "O love,/That thou couldst see my wars today. . . ." And he returns in the same mood from what we know is but a respite from certain defeat. He greets her: "O thou day o' the world."

And she greets him in language no less hyperbolic: "O infinite virtue, comest thou smiling from /The world's great snare uncaught?" That will be their final struggle—to remain uncaught by the world's great snare—even while defeat, humiliation, and death stare them in the face, even while Antony slips momentarily into recrimination. Looking out from their love-created dream world, they see the world of Caesar as an alien and malign power, with which no compromise is possible, and from which their only escape is death.

The respite is soon over. A fresh battle brings complete and certain defeat, and Antony reverts for the moment to his old self. Though he imputes to Cleopatra a literal betrayal, he is really raging against the love which has made him other than he once was. We can perceive this in his juxtaposing his loss, his love, and the charge of betrayal.

> The hearts
> That spanieled me at heels, to whom I gave
> Their wishes, do discandy, melt their sweets
> On blossoming Caesar; and this pine is barked,
> That overtopped them all. Betrayed I am,
> O this false soul of Egypt! this grave charm—
> Whose eye becked forth my wars and called them home,
> Whose bosom was my crownet, my chief end—
> Like a right gypsy hath at fast and loose
> Beguiled me to the very heart of loss! (IV.xii.20-29)

To suppose that Cleopatra packed cards with Caesar would be absurd. But, though Antony is rationalizing, there is more truth in his sense of betrayal than we may initially be inclined to credit. In a sense she *has* betrayed him. For from the point of view of self-regarding reason, any commitment made for love "betrays" the self's freedom. To the proud, the power of love does really seem to be a kind of bewitchment.

At the same time Antony is undergoing a final change. His speech now conveys his own awareness of passing from one state of being to another. The "melting" imagery, clustered thickly here, signifies a melting in Antony's soul:

> Sometime we see a cloud that's dragonish . . .
> That which is now a horse, even with a thought
> The rack dislimns . . .
> My good knave Eros, now thy Captain is
> Even such a body. Here I am Antony;
> Yet cannot hold this visible shape . . . (IV.xiv.2,9-10,12-14)

He thus reaches his ultimate personal status to which he has all along been moving. He receives the news of Cleopatra's death calmly, and his rage will not return, even when he learns that she really played him false in this. Now he yearns toward death:

> Unarm me, Eros. The long day's task is done,
> And we must sleep. (35-36)

And now "all labour/Mars what it does; yea, very force entangles/Itself with strength." It is right that he should botch his suicide, for he is no more a soldier, no longer part of the world of force. He has entered the dream world of love where the truth of the actual world does not matter. In the sleep of death he will rejoin the partner of his dream:

> I come, my Queen . . . Stay for me.
> Where souls do couch on flowers, we'll hand in hand,
> And with our sprightly port make the ghosts gaze. (50-52)

When Antony dies in her arms, Cleopatra echoes the tone of this speech. Loving more deeply than we would have thought possible, she shares the mortal lot of all lovers:

> No more, but e'en a woman, and commanded
> By such poor passion as the maid that milks
> And does the meanest chares. (IV.xv.73-75)

It is this very participation in common mortality that makes her, paradoxically, a lass unparalleled, more royal than any queen. It enables her to tell the gods "This world did equal theirs/Till they had stolen our jewel." She will seek to regain that world. Assuming a vestige of Antony's manhood, she will do it after the high Roman fashion and make death proud to take her.

Those who assume a moralistic view of the play ought to find the whole fifth act superfluous. The lust-ridden Antony has already died his fool's death—what sort of climax can occur after that? Actually, the last act makes an impression of extraordinary "rightness" and power. We of course expect to see Cleopatra join Antony in death. But more than that, we expect the manifold themes of the play to be brought into precise focus and given final statement.

Such a final vision is epitomized by Cleopatra in one of the most compressed and eloquent passages of the play:

>   'Tis paltry to be Caesar.
> Not being Fortune, he's but Fortune's knave,
> A minister of her will. And it is great
> To do that thing that ends all other deeds,
> Which shackles accidents and bolts up change,
> Which sleeps, and never palates more the dung,
> The beggar's nurse and Caesar's. (V.ii.2-8)

Subject always to accident and change, Caesar will never be better off than a beggar. But by her suicide Cleopatra will forever shackle accidents and bolt up change—she will attain, in short, a state of eternal immutability. In loving each other as persons, in the full development of their mortal natures, the lovers have in a sense transcended their mortality; they have made for each other a world that stands outside of time and is therefore changeless, eternal.

As early as I.v, Cleopatra had longed to "sleep out this great gap of time/My Antony is away." Now the association of love with dreaming and timelessness, with death and immortality, becomes insistent. "I dreamed there was an Emperor Antony," she tells Dolabella. "Oh, such another sleep, that I might see/But such another man." And she goes on to describe an Antony who never was: "His legs bestrid the ocean: his reared arm/Crested the world. . . ." Only the person who lived and had her being in that private world can know how true a dream it was, for it was true only for her. So, when she asks him if "there was, or might be, such a man/As this I dreamt of," Dolabella replies: "Gentle madam, no." "You lie," she cries, "up to the hearing of the gods." And in the light of the truth only she can know, he does lie.

Only in the sleep of death can she return to her dream. That is why the distinction between mortality and immortality now begins to blur—the words have now become virtually synonymous. To be mortal (i.e., human) is to be capable of immortality; to be subject to death (mortal) is to be endowed with the capacity for transcendence. Just as there is a shackling of accidents in love, so there is a bolting up of change in death. What we happen to believe about such matters outside the play does not matter. In the dreamy ambience of these last scenes, we believe for the moment in the lover's intimation that there is forever and forever in love. It is as though the dream, now "past the size of dreaming," has suddenly become real, and the actual world is itself but a dream.

This is why the clown passage is so dazzling. Its mood is almost playful—a solemn merriment, as before a momentous and terrible, yet eagerly longed-for, event. The Clown's malapropisms are never quite malaprop. His worm's biting is immortal. And those "that do die of it do seldom or never recover." *Mortal* and *immortal*—both meanings are there—the universal condition of men, and the condition the lovers aspire to. And "this is most falliable, the worm's an odd worm," not to be trusted "but in the keeping of wise people." An odd worm indeed—very like the strange serpent which Antony described for Lepidus; a multifoliate symbol: of mortality and immortality, of human love and of the dung out of which it breeds, of death, which shackles accidents and bolts up change. "I wish you joy o' the worm," says the clown. And Cleopatra expects no less of the worm, for she has immortal longings in her.

She goes to death eagerly—as to her lover. "The stroke of death is as a lover's pinch,/Which hurts, and is desired." Yet her death is no Wagnerian *Liebestod*: there is in it no hint of flight from the body or loss of personal identity. "If she first meet the curled Antony," she says of Iras, "He'll make demand of her, and spend that kiss/Which is my Heaven to have." Cleopatra hastens to prevent her. And in the now fully realized world of the play, we see her last as one asleep and dreaming,

> As she would catch another Antony
> In her strong toil of grace. (V.ii.350-51)

The play is surely not a tragedy in any usual sense. In Aristotelian terms it fails to qualify. It is the imitation of a serious action, its protagonists are noble but imperfect. But they do not pass from happiness to misery; rather they pass from an indeterminate state to one of complete happiness. That is so, at any rate, in terms of the play's own value system— to which we are obliged to submit. Our response to Cleopatra's death (which I have tried to describe) does not involve pity and fear. It rather comprises a joyful exhilaration in the attainment of perfect fulfillment of desire, in the release from the limits of mortal existence. Such an effect puts the play quite outside the tragic genre—as that genre has traditionally been conceived.

An important condition for the creation of this peculiar effect is the belief, brilliantly realized in the play, that, for true lovers, death is not a terrible event, the end of personal existence. It is rather a dark entryway to a truer and higher kind of life, the way to immortality. This is Cleopatra's own view of her death, and the play's eloquence makes us, at least for the imaginative moment, share it. Antony's death at the end of act IV is, of course, pitiful, almost pathetic. But his death is only a stage in the action of the play, not its culmination. No longer part of the world of force, a lover more than a soldier, Antony dies no longer striving for what we now see as valueless. We ought to regard his death, therefore, as a parting of lovers, and not as the miserable fall of greatness. Antony himself, we may recall, anticipates in death a reunion with his beloved.

All this may sound very romantic or mystical. Yet the play's vision is not one of which any romantic poet was capable; it is precise and profound rather than vague and diffuse. As for its mysticism, I can only say that it is there in the play and that it has affinities with the mysticism of Christianity at which we are not wont to boggle. The intuition that love transcends time, that it tends toward both death and immortality—these beliefs seem to be rooted in the race, as a vast body of love poetry, both secular and divine, attests. Christianity tells a more complex story of life beyond death, of the Love which leads to it. And the Christian story draws many of its analogues from the natural experience of lovers.

If we come to *Antony and Cleopatra* expecting the tragic form familiar to us from Shakespeare's other tragedies, we are bound to be disappointed.[5] Antony, we will feel, is not so impressive a tragic figure as Lear or Othello. His nobility is largely conveyed by poetic eloquence, and his weakness verges on vice. Moreover, he dies in hugger-mugger, almost farcically. And Cleopatra—can we take seriously such a wanton?

If, however, we see that the play has its own peculiar form (what shall we call it? a secular mystery play?), we will not so misinterpret it. We will see that it is not an immoral play, and that to raise such questions about it is to betray one's (mistaken) presuppositions about its form. There is, of course, a good and evil in the play; but these cannot be assumed to be the same as ethical categories outside the play. The good in the play is what the lovers choose: love and death and immortality. The evil is what they reject: self-love and the "rational" world of Caesar, which is subject to fortune and passes away. These are the good and evil of the work itself, the "imaginative" good, which, as Wilson Knight puts it, will often correspond roughly

to the ethical 'good': but . . . we must be prepared to modify our ethical response till it is in tune with our imaginative vision. That does not mean that we must exclude ethical considerations. But we must use ethical phraseology in subjection to imaginative effects, as part of our interpretation of the imaginative whole.[6]

Wilson Knight's advice applies preeminently to *Antony and Cleopatra*, whose form is anomalous, and whose meaning is mystical or metaphysical rather than ethical. My own feeling about the play is that, when Shakespeare came to write it, near the close of his career, he was for once writing entirely for himself rather than for his audience; that, looking back like St. Thomas over his work, he felt that it was all but straw; that the values which had figured importantly in all his earlier work—kingship and honor, worldly success and power—that these were in the eye of eternity but so many dreams; and that true love between a man and a woman— imperfect and mortal though they be—is worth more than all the rest.

That Shakespeare should have arrived at such a vision is the less surprising in the light of his early thematic interests. From the Sonnets on, as we have seen, Shakespeare was deeply concerned with love and death, with time and immortality, with the conflict between love and lust, between the values of kingship and soldiership and those that are private, personal, and merely human. The pessimism about heterosexual love, which is implicit in the Sonnets, explicit in *Hamlet, Troilus,* and *Othello,* begins to alter and diminish in *King Lear*, anticipating in a way the transcendent humanism of *Antony and Cleopatra*. There flesh and spirit meet in a harmonious and mystical union; there the mortal and merely human transcends itself. This was the vision which required the creation of a new and nameless genre, of which *Antony and Cleopatra* is the only instance.

Shakespeare's development before *Antony* makes comprehensible his creating such a play at such a point in his career. What seems unlikely—what seems indeed astonishing—is that he should have dared to use for such a play the story of an aging and dissolute soldier and a licentious Egyptian queen.

CHAPTER EIGHT

THE WINTER'S TALE

So much of Shakespeare has been "christened" in our time that it is not surprising to find *The Winter's Tale* interpreted (in S. L. Bethell's words) as an allegory of Christian doctrine about sin, grace, and salvation.[1] Our reading of *Antony and Cleopatra* and the progress we have so far traced make it seem unlikely that Shakespeare should have produced near the end of his career such an explicitly Christian play. If there are Christian meanings in *Antony*, these are surely mere overtones, poetic extensions of generally available ideas which Shakespeare used for his own ends. In both *Antony* and *King Lear* there are non-Christian and indeed heretical attitudes. It is precisely these "heresies" which, it appears to me, are carried forward into *The Winter's Tale* and *Pericles*.

Though he too suggests a more Christian view than I think the play will support, G. Wilson Knight's description of *The Winter's Tale* as a myth of immortality comes very close to the truth (though much depends on how one construes "myth" and "immortality").[2] Knight brings us, in any case, face to face with the central issue of any study of the play: What is its mode of reality? It is a strange play, quite melodramatic, full of arbitrary action and obscure motivation; yet it brims with a kind of super-reality, with intimations of a transcendent and supremely real world, existing beneath or beyond the shadowy literal one.

Compared to Othello's jealousy, Leontes' seems absurd. Othello, for one thing, has his Iago, a diabolical figure, a kind of projection of the egotism inherent in human nature and human love. One sees, therefore, in Othello's fall, not psychological realism, but a measure of plausibility, a connection between character, situation, and event. Leontes, on the other hand, has no Iago. Furthermore, there is in *The Winter's Tale* neither the careful characterization of Leontes nor the delineation of his wooing and personal relation to his beloved—all of which we find in *Othello*. So that, whereas we feel a certain comprehensibility in the terrible course of Othello's and Desdemona's lives, we have a sense of absurdity, of utter madness, in the sudden onset and awful consequence of Leontes' passion.

And yet it is well for us to remember that at its deepest level of meaning, *Othello* is the story of the *causelessness* of evil, that ultimately Othello's jealousy *has* no cause—even though we are dramatically convinced of its reality and, yes, its inevitability. So there is more similarity between the two cases than at first appears. Apart from differences consequent upon genre, the most emphatic difference between the two jealousies lies in this: rather than developing by stages, Leontes' jealousy is full-blown at its inception. (At any rate, we have no reason to believe that it existed before we first notice it in the play.) This combination of peremptory and realistic presentation points to the play's peculiar nature. Since we are convinced of the truth of Leontes' passion but unable to account for it in a realistic way—in terms of psychological or real antecedents—we are led to infer a level of dramatic action other than the literal one. And this inference is supported by a number of other features of the play.

One of the most interesting of these is what I should call "emphatic digression." We get throughout the play passages that have no immediate dramatic function but are given unquestionable prominence. One of them occurs in the first scene of the play. The scene is a simple expository one, presenting the situation (the long visit of Polixenes, the long-standing love between the royal friends) and concluding with this "digression":

> *Arc.* . . . You have an unspeakable comfort of your young
> Prince Mamillius. It is a gentleman of the greatest promise that
> ever came into my note.
> *Cam.* I very well agree with you in the hopes of him. It is a
> gallant child; one that indeed physics the subject, makes old
> hearts fresh. They that went on crutches ere he was born desire
> yet their life, to see him a man.
> *Arc.* Would they else be content to die?
> *Cam.* Yes; if there were not other excuse why they should
> desire to live.
> *Arc.* If the King had no son, they would desire to live on
> crutches till he had one. (I.i.42-50)

The hope set on the young prince prepares of course for his death. But there is clearly more than this in the passage. The (apparently digressive) longing of old citizens to see the prince survive–to carry on regime and race–is a longing for a kind of immortality. Similar passages with similar implications serve to develop both our awareness of an extra-literal meaning in the play and the meaning itself. Here are a few of them:

> Thou met'st with things dying, I with things newborn (III.iii.116)

> These your unusual weeds to each part of you
> Do give a life–no shepherdess, but Flora
> Peering in April's front! (IV.iv.1-3)

> Would I were dead, but that methinks already–
> What was he that did make it? See, my lord,
> Would you not deem it breathed? and that those veins
> Did verily bear blood? (V.iii.62-64)

Each of these passages, in various degrees, conveys meanings which the dramatic context–the literal one–does not support. We are therefore compelled to see the play in terms of latent rather than ostensible action. This process is involved, as I have already suggested, in the handling of the most crucial event of the play: the onset of Leontes' jealousy. Here, in fact, we may discern a complex set of latent connections.

Shortly before the outbreak of Leontes' jealousy, we get several curious emphases. There is, first, Leontes' own insistence that Polixenes remain in Sicilia. Why, we wonder, does he urge the very thing that suspicion should oppose? Then, just after Polixenes agrees to stay, comes the emphatic digression on the boyhood of the two kings. "We were," says Polixenes, "Two lads that thought there was no more behind/But such a day tomorrow as today,/And to be boy eternal." In brief: just before the onset of adult, sexually grounded evil–a passion both unmotivated and irrepressible–we are told nostalgically of the idyllic, asexual, brotherly love of the boy-kings. And this idyllic form of life is connected with immortality. The implication here is not that boys do not think about death, but that their being occurs in a timeless realm and, further, that boyhood conveys intimations of immortality which dissolve with age. Childhood, the period before sexual maturity, is connected with goodness and (sexual) purity and immortality. Maturity, on the other hand, is emphatically linked with sexuality, with evil, and with death.

Yet we cannot but recall here the apparently innocuous passage in the first scene where the aged subjects express their longing for the coming-to-manhood of their young prince. In the present digression on their boyhood, Polixenes goes on to describe those golden days in detail, focusing now on the purity and innocence which he clearly implies has since been lost:

> What we changed
> Was innocence for innocence; we knew not
> The doctrine of ill-doing, nor dreamed
> That any did. (I.ii.68-71)

Boyhood is thus given a theological status. It is equivalent to the prelapsarian state of Adam, and it carries with it the perfection of being and joy (and immortality?) which was Adam's. Polixenes goes on, regretfully, just slightly whimsical, to speak of the "fall" that has since occurred:

> Had we pursued that life,
> And our weak spirits n'er been higher reared
> With stronger blood, we should have answered heaven
> Boldly, "Not guilty," the imposition cleared
> Hereditary ours. (71-74)

What is most curious and surprising about this is the almost bawdy reach of the allusions: clearly "spirits" and "blood" have sexual (and along with "higher reared," phallic) meanings here. These meanings are insisted on when Hermione picks them up and, rather playfully, develops Polixenes' more serious thought. "By this we gather/You have tripped since." Polixenes replies:

> O my most sacred lady,
> Temptations have since then been born to 's; for
> In those unfledged days was my wife a girl;
> Your precious self had then not crossed the eyes
> Of my young playfellow. (76-79)

Their tripping is clearly sexual; and the temptations have been *borne* to them in the form of their wives—with whom, as Hermione notes in her playful rejoinder, the princes first "sinned."

The whole passage is charming, but it carries a serious set of implications. It reinforces the already intimated theme of youthful innocence corrupted by age and sexuality, and, making use of Christian theological "extensions" it suggests the close connection between maturity, sexuality, corruption, and death. Only a few moments later (at line 108), we are surprised by Leontes' sudden (sexual) passion, depicted with great conviction but ostensibly unmotivated. Given the context so far described, we would not, however, need to be very sophisticated Freudians to perceive a latent motive for Leontes' jealousy—especially since we are made emphatically aware that Leontes yearns for Hermione's betrayal with Polixenes both before and after the outbreak. ("How thou lovest us show in our brother's welcome," he tells her.) Early, idyllic, male, asexual, innocent love; the "fall" into sexual maturity and marriage; then mad, unconsciously moti- vated passion: a jealousy which has the appearance of madness to all rational observers but which seems irresistible and in some sense "natural."

That Leontes' passion is at once abnormal and natural is suggested also by Hermione's unwittingly accurate remark—"My life stands in the level of your dreams"—to which Leontes replies: "Your actions are my dreams" (III.ii.82,83). And the dreamlike reality of Leontes' passion and its terrible consequences, supremely real and supremely nightmarish, become ever more closely identified with the unreal/real quality of the whole play, a winter's tale that is continually calling attention to its fantastic status.

When (at I.ii.163) Leontes asks Polixenes if he is as fond of his "young Prince as we/Do seem to be of ours," Polixenes replies:

> He makes a July's day short as December,
> And with his varying childness cures in me
> Thoughts that would thick my blood.   (I.ii.169-71)

We may take it that the children of both kings stand in similar relation to their fathers—much loved, rejoiced in, doted on. We may assume also that Polixenes' final remark applies to both fathers—but what exactly does it mean? What are the thoughts which would thick the blood? And how does the boy "cure" them? If we keep in mind the suggestions we noted earlier of the connection between boyhood and immortality, we may discern a clear set of similar relations here. The "thoughts that would thick my blood" are thoughts of death. Having passed, like Leontes, into the period of physical maturity, Polixenes is oppressed, like Leontes, with the sense of age and approaching death—for which the only cure is his son's "varying childness." Thus, both kings sense in their children (and we are becoming intensely aware of this) their means of defeating death; they are, like their subjects, "physicked" by their children—their old hearts are made fresh by them.

"Thoughts that would thick my blood"—that phrase hints at another latent motive for Leontes' apparent madness: death-obsessed, he madly aims at the very accomplishment of the end that terrifies. There is a sort of mad logic in this (as in the suicide), for with death comes an end to the terror of death. So, too, we are now prepared for the precise consequence of his persistence in madness. A daughter, "a goodly babe," is born, and Leontes casts it from him as he does his wife, another pearl. And so the very means to his immortality is cast away. The oracle speaks truly: "the King shall live without an heir if that which is lost be not found." When Leontes rejects the oracle, we hear immediately that the prince is dead. A few moments later, Hermione dies. What is lost is Leontes' wife and children. But his hope is also lost, and he will live without hope until he finds what is lost—not just Perdita and Hermione—but his innocence, his childhood. The rest of the play will show us the finding of what was lost, not only literally, but—is not the word just?—anagogically.

All along, however, we are given presages of the happy issue of all this. Leontes himself suddenly regains his senses on hearing that his son has died; it is as though the actuality of death—what has unconsciously motivated his frenzy—is what is needed to bring him back to sanity. Then, in the next scene (III.iii), there is Antigonus' strange account of Hermione's apparition to him—"ne'er was dream/So like a waking." This not only hints at her return to life at the end, but prepares us for Perdita's survival and her eventual "finding." Hermione instructs Antigonus to leave the babe in Bohemia and

> for the babe
> Is counted lost forever, Perdita
> I prithee call't.   (III.iii.32-34)

Perdita is not lost forever, but "counted" so. And then Hermione foretells the death of Antigonus (which we will see in a moment, when he exits pursued by a bear) and so certifies her prophetic power. Watching the scene—Antigonus leaving the defenseless babe ("Blossom, speed thee well!" he says) and then himself about to be killed by the bear—we get the impression that unknown powers are at work, working to bring about the death of Antigonus and the survival of the blossom Perdita.

At such a moment—what would in another play be a moment of stark terror—comes the buffoonery of the Shepherd and his clownish son. The Clown describes the terrible sinking of the ship and the death of Antigonus, and there is the babe, miraculously saved. "Now bless thyself. Thou met'st with things dying, I with things newborn." A new movement in the mysterious pattern of these events is about to begin.

Though the change is prepared for, it is yet so great an alteration of tone that it astonishes us. After the irrepressible trickery of Autolycus, comes a scene of, not merely pastoral, but Edenic innocence and joyousness. It is the world hinted at in Polixenes' phrase "boy eternal"—the world of the pure heart's desire, where love is perfect and forever and there is no death. Though we did not learn his name, we have heard of Florizel before as the child who cures in Polixenes "thoughts that would thick my blood"; and here is the "blossom" Perdita, cast away and yet miraculously preserved. In a sense, we know already, then, that what was lost has been or will be found. And the tone tells us further that we are mysteriously returning to that world of childhood which Polixenes recalled nostalgically in the first act. Yet Perdita and Florizel are not children; they are young lovers who have retained, miraculously, the purity and joy of childhood.

The love of Florizel may be idyllic, but it is not platonic or wanting in passion. It is fully human and physical and rooted in sex—but it is uncorrupted and pure, without, as it were, the taint of concupiscence. And this is conveyed to us by the lovely lines he speaks to Perdita:[3]

> What you do
> Still betters what is done. When you speak, sweet,
> I'ld have you do it ever. When you sing,
> I'ld have you buy and sell so; so give alms;
> Pray so; and for the ordering your affairs,
> To sing them too. When you dance, I wish you
> A wave o' th' sea, that you might ever do
> Nothing but that; move still, still so,
> And own no other function. Each your doing,
> So singular in each particular,
> Crowns what you are doing in the present deed,
> That all your acts are queens. (IV.iv.135-46)

Her feeling for him is similarly passionate and pure: she will, she says, strew him with flowers

> Not like a corse; or if—not to be buried,
> But quick, and in mine arms. (131-132)

Though they are not children, they still have the power of making old hearts fresh. Both Camillo and Polixenes testify to this power in Perdita. "I should leave grazing," says Camillo, "were I of your flock,/And only live by gazing." And Polixenes remarks that "Nothing she does or seems/But smacks of something greater than herself,/Too noble for this place." This passage not only points to the hidden truth that Perdita is a real princess; it also serves to develop the sense of Perdita's dual status in the scene. When Florizel tells Perdita how in his lover's eyes she is a goddess, he is at once expressing his love and imputing a status to her which we can never be sure she does not truly possess.

No shepherdess, but Flora
Peering in April's front! This your sheepshearing
Is as a meeting of the petty gods,
And you the queen on't. (IV.iv.2-4)

We will never be quite sure whether Perdita is princess and disguised shepherdess, or Flora, or both at once. Even Perdita is conscious of strange
metamorphoses. "Sure this robe of mine/Does change my disposition."

In any case, this blossom, this shepherdess, this goddess of flowers and
nature, dispenses flowers to those celebrating the feast. To each age she
gives the flower that best becomes it—and thus expresses a deeper and
more affecting meaning than any country ritual would ever warrant. To
Camillo she gives rosemary and rue, which keep "Seeming and savor all the
winter long." To Polixenes she gives flowers "of middle summer." And so
to the others. This queen of curds and cream who "smacks of something
greater than herself" will bring young Doricles "that/Which he not dreams
of." The whole scene is a miracle of poetry—conveying meaning on various levels, and carrying forward themes foreshadowed in the darker first
part of the play. Giving to each age its appropriate flower—i.e., its proper
"fruition," fulfillment, joy—Perdita (Flora) thus ritually signifies a perfection of being—an "adequation" of form to function in human being.
And this signifies fruition in all ages and conditions of men, since it is
celebrated by a fully human Perdita (who is also a divine being) and
shadows forth a vision of human perfection, of an immortality rooted in
nature itself. And this, of course, picks up the Wordsworthian hints at
immortality of the first act.

In Polixenes' violent anger at his son and rancor at Perdita we also get
a reprise of Leontes' "fall." Just as *we* could see the truth about Hermione, so now *we* see (what Florizel does not) that Perdita is the lost princess, not a shepherdess; and *we* see what passion-blinded Polixenes does
not see: not only that the lovely shepherdess is a true princess and that
she is *naturally* noble, that all her acts are queens, but that she is touched
with divinity. In rejecting Perdita, then, Polixenes gainsays the evidence of
his own perceptions—it is he who notes that she "smacks of something
greater than herself"—and loses, as Leontes before him lost, his hope and
his means to immortality. Ironically, he refers explicitly to this in his ad-
juration to his son to consult his father, "all whose joy is nothing else/ But
fair posterity." And there is irony, too, in his contradicting his views on
hybrid breeding (at IV.iv.88ff.).

Florizel's fresh and exhilarating passion, at once sexual and pure, and
Perdita's frank and wholesome love for him, seem to be in part a renewal
of the boy eternal theme. But it also constitutes a modification of that

theme in that the lovers are not children but young adults who have come to maturity and to full sexual love *without* corruption. They have carried over to maturity the joyful perfection of childhood with its intimations of immortality. And when we know that the lovers will repair to Sicilia, we can foretell the joy in the offing—for we have already been led to anticipate that what was lost will be found.

In a well-known (and apparently quite digressive) passage to which I have already alluded, Perdita and Polixenes dispute the relative merits of art and nature in the breeding of flowers. Perdita takes a conservative position against hybridization of species; Polixenes takes a progressive or humanist one, defending art as itself a part of nature:

> . . . nature is made better by no mean
> But nature makes that mean. So, over that art
> Which you say adds to nature, is an art
> That nature makes. . . .
> This is an art
> Which does mend nature—change it rather, but
> The art itself is nature. (IV.iv.89-92;95-97)

Edward Tayler has traced the origin and the development of these concepts from Plato to the Renaissance. He shows that, especially in the Renaissance, the art/nature distinction was a pervasive one, affecting thought in ethics, politics, education, literary theory, etc. Tayler also points out the importance of the distinction especially for pastoral literature, and he makes a case for its being a formative theme in *The Winter's Tale.*[4]

Now, it seems to me that Tayler overstates his case a good deal. *The Winter's Tale* has obvious pastoral features, but these are, as it were, taken for granted; they are not at the center of interest in this play—as they are, for example, in *As You Like It*. Similarly, the playful and mildly derisive quality of *As You Like It*, its gentle satire of both courtly and rural ideals, is only dimly present in *The Winter's Tale*—where, as our discussion should already have made clear, Shakespeare has other fish to fry. With the nature/art pairing, again the "standard" relations between these concepts are assumed; but Shakespeare's main interest in them is unusual, one might say, peculiar. It is an interest that goes all the way back to the Sonnets, and one which persists throughout his career. I am referring to the connection between art and immortality and the parallel connection between nature and immortality. The clues that lead in this direction have already been noted: the latency of meaning in the play, the hints at immortality) to be attained in despite of evil passion and death) the improbable (or miracle play) plot, involving the loss of childhood innocence and child and what these signify, and the predictable finding of these again. And all of this bound up, as it were, in a play whose "artistry" is set emphatically before our minds.

In an extraordinary essay on *"Cymbeline* and Coterie Dramaturgy," Arthur C. Kirsch makes some remarks about the structure of so-called coterie drama and its models which are very much to the point here. Taking the tragicomedies of Beaumont and Fletcher as representative, he remarks that the most distinguishing feature of their works

is its deliberate self-consciousness. Beaumont and Fletcher's plays, like all plays, are designed to have an audience, but unlike plays at the Globe their effect depends upon the audience's consciousness of the means by which it is moved.[5]

In *The Winter's Tale*, as we have already seen, there is a good deal which is (in Kirsch's words) "insistently and consciously theatrical"—though Kirsch does not take up our play. And this theatricality is used to convey a sense of latent action and meaning. But there is more to it than this. The deliberate "artistry," the dramaturgy which calls attention to itself, serves further to make the audience aware of the distinction between drama and reality, between fiction and life, between art and nature.[6]

But it is not only these distinctions as such that Shakespeare aims at. He is even more concerned with the awareness which these serve to promote: the awareness that the play itself is a piece of art which in some sense is indistinguishable from nature. We have something of this awareness in the ironies that proliferate in the passage referred to above (IV.iv.89-97). Here Perdita, apparently a bit of "wild stock," aspires to marry a "gentler scion." Polixenes approves of such a marriage in the world of flowers, but he quickly changes his tune when he discovers that Perdita intends to marry his son. The irony is doubled, of course, by our knowing that the shepherdess is really a princess, a product of centuries of careful breeding and culture—an art which is part of nature, as is the breeding of hybrid flowers.

Perdita, then, is a "bud of nobler race" and also a goddess of nature—so Shakespeare's own art intimates.

No shepherdess, but Flora
Peering in April's front. (IV.iv.2-3)

Nothing she does or seems
But smacks of something greater than herself,
Too noble for this place. (157-59)

Shepherdess, princess, goddess—all three at once she is, and her being so equivocal a being hints that nature "contains" her in her various aspects. And this impression is itself produced by Shakespeare's art, performed before us on this artificial stage, conveying a sense of nature at her most wondrous. His art is part of nature, then, in two senses. The Perdita who "plays" Flora is and is not Flora, just as the boy who plays Perdita is and is not Perdita. That is the miracle of Shakespeare's art: it makes believe, and what it makes us believe is true. And Shakespeare's art is also a "mean" which nature makes, since the images he creates are mined out of nature's own quarry and the human mind.

Moreover, the play is a fiction, a work of art, which pretends to *be* nature. And the aspect of nature which it imitates—the action of the play— has to do with the natural cycle of birth and death and regeneration, or, more precisely, with the emergence from and return to the transcendent world beyond time, the world of eternity. Of all this the poet's art is an embodiment—it is "an artifice of eternity." But it also becomes part of the natural world; it is an expression of the eternal which is implicit in the transitory. "The art itself is nature."

Our play tells a miraculous story of the loss of child and wife, of their being found again, brought back from death to life—of an heir being found who will, through "breed," bring immortality to the king and survival to the race. That the heir is such a means is suggested by persistent allusions in V.i. When Cleomenes and Dion suggest that the king should marry again, Paulina opposes them. The gods, she says, "Will have fulfilled their secret purposes." And to Leontes: "Care not for issue;/The crown will find an heir." She has faith in the gods and she teaches Leontes to have faith. And *we* are led to anticipate not only a happy issue, but a fulfillment. Paulina is also hinting at the climactic miracle of Hermione's return from death—here and at several points throughout the scene. She makes Leontes vow not to marry

> Unless another,
> As like Hermione as is her picture,
> Affront his eye.   (V.i.73-75)

If he does marry again, Paulina will choose his queen.

> She shall not be so young
> As was your former; but she shall be such
> As, walked your first Queen's ghost, it should take joy
> To see her in your arms.   (78-81)

At her bidding, Leontes will not marry until "your first Queen's again in breath."

When, a moment later, Perdita and Florizel arrive, they have become figures of immortality, real and symbolic:

> And your fair princess—goddess! O, alas,
> I lost a couple that 'twixt heaven and earth
> Might thus have stood begetting wonder, as
> You, gracious couple, do! (131-34)

Leontes does not know it yet, but we can see that what was lost is about to be found, that not just Perdita but the lost Mamillius will also be found in Florizel. And this gracious couple bring with them—even Leontes seems to sense this—a return of the golden life of "boy eternal." Leontes says to Florizel:

> Your mother was most true to wedlock, Prince,
> For she did print your royal father off,
> Conceiving you. Were I but twenty-one,
> Your father's image is so hit in you,
> His very air, that I should call you brother,
> As I did him, and speak of something wildly
> By us performed before. (124-30)

The first part of the double climax is reported in the next scene. We learn that the oracle is fulfilled, the king's daughter is found. Nothing but wondrous events, "so like an old tale that the verity of it is in strong suspicion." And then, even before the report of the divinely foretold events has been concluded, we are prepared for the second part of the climax. We hear about a work of art, a statue of Hermione by that "rare Italian master, Julio Romano, who, had he himself eternity and could put breath into his work, would beguile Nature of her custom, so perfectly he is her ape." Having seen "great creating Nature" perform her miracle of "ransoming" the world, we are now about to see how art, the ape of nature, performs her own sort of miracle, one that will occur before our very eyes and thus enact the deepest meaning of our play.

The revival of Hermione will not be a complete surprise. There is, in this final scene, an odd sort of equivocation about the statue—not unlike the equivocation about Perdita's divinity in the sheepshearing festival. As a result, when we perceive that the statue is alive, we are both startled and deeply moved. What makes the scene so deeply moving in the performance is just its profound meaning—for Leontes *and* for us. For Leontes, the return to life of Hermione is a finding of what was lost, an attainment of his heart's deepest desire. What makes this possible is his passage through a spiritual fall and regeneration, his contrition and suffering and purified love. Gazing rapt at the statue, Leontes pleads with Paulina not to draw the curtain:

> Let be, let be!
> Would I were dead, but that methinks already— (V.iii.61-62)

It is a curious speech: either he is saying that he would like to die so that he can be with Hermione, except that he thinks he is already dead; or, that he would like to die, except that he thinks Hermione is alive. I think the latter interpretation is preferable because it is a variation of the theme in the first scene, where the old desire to live only to see the prince a man.

The passage also points to the central meaning of the scene: that art, a mean which nature makes, is a mean of immortality. "The fixture of her eye," says Leontes, "has motion in 't/As we are mocked with art." But they are only apparently mocked with art. The statue is the living Hermione, and she is not, as we have been led to believe, created by the art of Romano. She is created by the art of William Shakespeare—as is the entire scene, by which we are both cozened and deeply moved. And the fact of our being so moved tells us that the fantastic story, the product of art, is true. Paulina tells Leontes: "It is required/That you do awake your faith." Yes, and that applies to us, too. So, at the end, our faith awakened, we believe in the miracle and in what it signifies.

If we stand back from the play for a moment, we can see, I think, how all its themes come together at the end. All that was lost is found. The love that was corrupted is purged and renewed. And art and nature are reconciled, both being means of attaining immortality—much as Plato explained the matter in the *Symposium*, And, as in Plato, the driving force behind both breed and art is love.

CHAPTER NINE

CONCLUSION

Each play of Shakespeare's is different from all the rest, each unique in structure and meaning. Yet through all his work there persists a central pattern of feeling and attitude. Amidst infinite variety, remarkable similarities and recurrences. It is precisely this pattern of similarities within differences which, along with purely formal features, marks Shakespeare's work as distinctively Shakespearean, and conveys to the reader a sense of personality in and behind the work.

This personality is, in fact, what we refer to when, as seems to me unavoidable, we speak of Shakespeare as at once the mind expressed in the work and, in some sense, the totality of the work itself. We cannot study the great body of his work without coming to a strong sense of a style that makes the work distinctive and all of a piece; at the same time, we cannot avoid the consciousness of a personality, of an interiority, expressed in and by the work as a whole.

When we refer to Shakespeare in this sense, we do not tumble into the biographical fallacy. For we are not then referring to the historical Shakespeare at all—the man who ate and drank, married, acted in plays, bought houses, etc. Nor are we referring to Shakespeare the artist, who is also an (abstracted) historical person. We are rather referring to a distinctive, ideal (i.e., mentally existent) being, which we project from Shakespeare's total work understood as a coherent set of discrete, integrally related parts. In this sense, "Shakespeare" is precisely the name we need to refer to the works by which we know him and to which his presence is a constantly necessary source of illumination. If this is so, it gives a fresh meaning to the ancient notion of literary immortality which our author so fondly utilized in the Sonnets.

Each play is different from all the rest; yet something of each is in all. When the poet-lover of the Sonnets says that his love is not "the child of state," not "subject to Time's love or to Time's hate," but that it "all alone stands hugely politic," he is expressing a view of life quite in accord with that implied in Bolingbroke's remark on learning of Richard's murder: "They love not poison that do poison need." The violation of his humanity incumbent upon the holder of power—the bitter and sad recognition of this—is implicit in that line, a complex of thought and feeling which is pervasive in Shakespeare. A little earlier in *Richard II* we have the best instance perhaps of Shakespeare's ubiquitous ambivalence toward kingship in Richard's soliloquy before his death. "But whate'er I be," Richard sums up,

> Nor I nor any man that but man is,
> With nothing shall be pleased till he be eased
> With being nothing. (V.v.39-41)

Richard's speech is in an earlier style than Hamlet's graveside ruminations, but the two passages have close affinities: in both there is a powerful sense of the all-engrossing power of time, of the vanity of worldy power, and (implicitly) the preciousness of life. Falstaff's response to Hal's parodic upbraiding—"Banish plump Jack, and banish all the world!"—is at once absurd and true, for in casting off that bag of guts, Hal is rejecting part of his own humanity.

These thematic oppositions, while persisting, themselves change in the course of Shakespeare's career. There are three "stages" in this change, roughly corresponding to the periods 1592-1600, 1601-06, and 1607-11 (approximately the periods suggested by Dowden a century ago). The first period contains all the later developments *in potentia;* there is a persistent ambivalence here, a sort of suspension of judgment. The Sonnets, obsessed with death, hint at survival, sometimes indeed assert it, but not consistently. What the Sonnets express most powerfully (aside from the sense of death's inexorable victory) is the intuition of love's transcendent value—which is, rather obscurely, related to the old idea of literary immortality.

In the Lancastrian histories, the ambivalence of the Sonnets takes a more political form: kingship, honor, soldiership, and the capacity for politic manipulation—these stand in continual opposition to the personal values of love and friendship, truthfulness and simple human decency. On the one side there are Richard Crookback and Bolingbroke and Hal; on the other, Richard II, Falstaff and (rather ambiguously) Hotspur. The conflict between love and honor, between the demands of feeling and "reason," is dramatized explicitly in *Julius Caesar*, the first of the mature tragedies.

The second period encompasses various sorts of revulsion: against the body and sexuality (foreshadowed in the bitter sonnets), against the traditional beliefs in a rational universe, and, in *Hamlet* and *Troilus*, against the very possibility of value in a world gone mad. In *Othello* we get, not disbelief in traditional values exactly, but a profound pessimism as to their realization in a flawed humanity. *King Lear* is in some ways the most crucial of the plays we have studied. In *Lear* we get the first movement away from the pessimism and skepticism of the works that precede it and toward the joyous vision of *Antony* and *The Winter's Tale*. There is no logical basis for Lear's perception that a beloved person is supremely valuable. His insight is a consequence of his recognition that he, like other "wretches," faces inevitable personal extinction. That is what teaches him his own need, to love and be loved. It is just this need—the intimation that love mitigates the horror of death—which presages the transcendent vision of the final plays.

In *Antony and Cleopatra* we reach the culmination of the Shakespearean "progress." (*The Winter's Tale* is a culmination of a different sort.) The most astonishing feature of *Antony* is the grounding of its action in a frankly sexual relationship between a pair of aging gamesters. The lovers' age brings into prominence the thematic relation between love and death, between mortality and immortality. It is just because they know how fast their precious minutes waste that they can rightly estimate the value of life and love. These lovers are not mastered by the blind god; in a sense he is their servant. That is why Cleopatra can approach death joyfully: by fully accepting her mortal nature, she paradoxically transcends it. The mortal worm whose biting is immortal "becomes" at last a baby at her breast that "sucks the nurse asleep," and it is loved because it brings death, which is, in the context, a transit to immortality.

The Winter's Tale is pervaded by a mellowed joyousness, an embracing of all that nature has conferred on erring humanity. There is also a kind of suppressed excitement, as of a religious celebrant just initiated into mysteries too wonderful for speech. This may be why the play is cast in the form of quasi-ritual: significant but unpragmatic action whose meaning is its only aim.

Florizel and Perdita, at once natural and divine creatures, enact a story about the transcendence of time *in* time. The play projects a vision— Wordsworthian or Blakean—of the beauty and divinity immanent in man, a vision intuited in childhood, lost in maturity, and ultimately recaptured. It is an old tale, but it becomes in Shakespeare's hands quite fresh again.

Something of the intuition of immortality which pervades *The Winter's Tale* was present, darkly, in the Sonnets. But the obsession with death has been dissipated and superseded by an intuition of survival, the feeling that all things shall be well. There is of course a hint of this feeling in the Sonnets:

> But thy eternal summer shall not fade . . . (18)

> Love alters not with his brief hours and weeks,
> But bears it out even to the edge of doom. . . . (116)

But we do not find in the Sonnets the acceptance of physical love, the happy union of flesh and spirit. True love is there expressed only for a young man, a love curiously purged of passion, while passion for the dark woman is mere lust and a source of misery for the poet. This separation of flesh and spirit is completely dissolved in *Antony*. In both *Antony* and *The Winter's Tale* there is a harmony of man's body and soul and a concomitant vision of immortality.

In *The Winter's Tale*, finally, we get an astonishing reprise of the eternizing themes of the Sonnets. As in the Sonnets, immortality is attained through both nature and art (breed and poetry). In the finding of Perdita and in her marriage to Florizel, the survival of regime and race is assured. As for literary immortality, Shakespeare here goes audaciously beyond any previous handling of the illusion and reality paradox. Hermione's return from death is no mere *coup de théâtre;* Shakespeare makes us believe both in Hermione's death and her revival. His dramatic art thus parallels the art of Julio Romano, "who had he himself eternity and could put breath into his work, would beguile Nature of her custom." Shakespeare *can* put breath into his work, and does indeed beguile nature of her custom. When Romano's statue comes to life, she is Shakespeare's creation entirely. And does she not breathe? So the fiction of the play is finally no fiction at all, but the deepest truth.

A fine index of the changes in Shakespeare's mind and art which have been wrought by time is provided by the contrast between Jaques's melancholy account of the ages of man and Perdita's distribution of appropriate flowers to young and old at the sheepshearing festival. There is nothing melancholy about the latter; there is only joy for every age, for all nature is now in harmony. Youth and age, male and female, love and the body—all oppositions are now reconciled in an all-embracing unity. And these reconcilements of opposites are reinforced by the formal (i.e., artistic) reconcilements of the play: the merging of comic and tragic modes, a style which combines the greatest apparent naturalness with quite "primitive" and emphatic device, the subtlest versification and apparently crude characterization. And how perfectly appropriate all this is in a play which is "like an old play still" but whose natural truth has tremendous depth and reach!

The play discovers the artifice of eternity in the very heart of Nature—in breed and art, which are natural products of a love in which body and spirit are one and inseparable. This is the final vision of the true love of the Sonnets. There, too, love was the source of the poet's creative power, but hung its head at the prospect of time and death. Here time is on the side of love, restores all losses, redeems the world. Here the object of the poet's love is neither a fair young man nor a dark woman, but nature herself and the human beings who are her most wonderful creations.

Freud and the Immortality Theme

Recent students of Freud hold that in *Beyond the Pleasure Principle* Freud radically changed his ideas about the basic human instincts. Recognizing that libido, the pleasure principle, ultimately becomes *thanatos* in the pursuit of the ultimate pleasure—which is nirvana or death—Freud posited, though confusedly, a life instinct, eros, whose nature it is to fight against the destructive tendency of thanatos and to lead the individual toward higher, more complex kinds of life. For Freud immortality was, of course, a delusion. Yet he seems to have discerned in the psyche a drive toward transcendence, much as Plato did two thousand years before him. In this, as in much else, Shakespeare seems to have anticipated Freud.

There is nothing very original about Freud's idea that the pleasure principle is ultimately destructive, suicidal. The classical, Christian, humanist idea that giving way to passion destroys the body and soul is the traditional view which Shakespeare adopts throughout his work. What is original in Freud is the notion that pleasure results from the reduction of tension and stimulation from without—so that the ultimate pleasure is death. In Shakespeare the ego-centered pursuit of passion or power enslaves one to time and so finally to death.

But in *Lear, Antony,* and *The Winter's Tale* there is a development analogous to what occurs in *Beyond the Pleasure Principle.* That is, in these plays there emerges an intuition of a transcendent eros. Unlike the Platonic eros and similar to the Freudian, it is closely allied with sexuality, involves body *and* soul. It is as though the pleasure principle and eros have merged, the energy of libido serving the aims of life rather than death.

In *Lear* it is the old man's discovery of the value of love which redeems the world's cruelty. In *Antony* there is an unequivocal vision of transcendence. The lovers' acceptance of their own mortal natures enables them to transcend the world of time. That is what makes Cleopatra a lass unparalleled, Caesar an ass unpolicied. And that is why she dies joyfully, anticipating a new heaven and earth. The asp is a mortal wretch and the baby at her breast; a figure of simple physical survival is thus transmuted into a figure of mortality and immortality at once, a figure of transcendence which is also an immanence.

In *The Winter's Tale* Leontes falls by betraying love. When he breaks the natural bonds which ground the survival of family, race, and regime, he loses the purity of boyhood and enters the time-world of jealousy and lust. Yet he finds again what was lost, and in the finding of daughter and wife, Leontes also finds his own immortality—or so the play powerfully intimates. There is also an astonishing resurgence of the art-eternizing theme: the play itself (we discern) is no illusion, but an image of the deepest truth, an eidolon of reality. That is a theme which has, of course, no counterpart in Freud.

"The Phoenix and Turtle"

It is now generally believed that the strange poem called "The Phoenix and Turtle" was written by Shakespeare—though this seems to be in part a result of its not being attributable to anyone else. Apart from the poem's strangely cryptic and abstract style—which is not a style to be found in Shakespeare or in any other Elizabethan poet—the poem is remarkable for its thought, at once profound, mystical, and philosophically sophisticated. If it can be shown that this thought is in accordance with Shakespeare's thematic development, as we have adumbrated it in this study, then, I think, we will have an additional reason for attributing the poem to Shakespeare. If, as I believe, the poem is Shakespeare's, an attempt at interpretation hardly needs justification.

Two recent essays on the poem have rightly emphasized the fact that Shakespeare's Phoenix, unlike everyone else's, is not reborn out of its own ashes.[1] This departure from a primary feature of the Phoenix myth, which would have startled a contemporary reader, has important ramifications for the overall meaning of the poem. I should like to point out some of these ramifications which have not, I think, received sufficient emphasis in interpreting the poem. But first let me clear away several minor points.

Though the poem celebrates the love of the Phoenix and the Turtle, it is ostensibly a funeral elegy. The praise of the two birds is part of the traditional eulogy for the dead. The subject of the poem is therefore not Truth or Beauty or any such abstraction; its subject is the death of the two lovers who are spoken of in the guise of the Phoenix and the Turtle. The poem is not, in short, a philosophical poem, though it makes use of philosophical terms and concepts in its "argument." Insufficient attention to these rather obvious points has tended to turn the poem, for some critics, into a metaphysical love poem rather than a funeral elegy. It has also tended to blur the relation between the poem's parts.

> Let the bird of loudest lay,
> On the sole Arabian tree,
> Herald sad and trumpet be,
> To whose sound chaste wings obey.

So the poem begins. Because his perch is the legendary Arabian tree of the Phoenix myth, some critics conclude that the "bird of loudest lay" is the Phoenix.[2] But a number of things make it clear that the herald is not the Phoenix. It is absurd, first of all, for the Phoenix to summon the mourners to her own funeral. What would there be to lament? It is, furthermore, quite appropriate for the herald (whatever his species) to be on the sole Arabian tree, for that is where the Phoenix has died and that is where her funeral will take place.

That the Phoenix has not revived is indicated rather emphatically at a number of points in the poem—in stanza 6,

> Love and constancy is dead,
> Phoenix and the turtle fled
> In a mutual flame from hence,

and in all five stanzas of the threnos. This sort of emphasis is hardly compatible with the view that the Phoenix has been reborn.[3] I do not think it very important that we know who the bird of "loudest lay" is, so long as we know it is not the Phoenix. That the herald is in fact the domestic cock is suggested in Ronald Bates's study of word and image associations in Shakespeare.[4] And bird lore tradition bears this out. Apart from the "natural" shrillness of its voice, the cock is traditionally associated with invoking good, and frightening away evil spirits—which is approximately its function in our poem.[5]

Much effort has been devoted to explicating the anthem (stanzas 6-13), the part of the poem which describes the paradoxical relationship between the Phoenix and the Turtle. As J. V. Cunningham has shown, this relationship is "modelled" on the relations of the three Persons of the Trinity as expounded by the scholastics.[6] This focus has tended to keep critical attention away from the connection between the anthem and the threnos. The poem contains no explicit connection between the two parts: the anthem describes the loving relation of the lovers; in the threnos Reason concludes the poem with a lamentation of the lovers' extinction, calling upon those that are true or fair to sigh a prayer at their urn.

In discussing the relation of the lovers to each other, Cunningham makes the important point that, though the lovers become one through love, they remain distinct persons. Human love "admits of no real identification. Though we desire it, if it were attained, one or both would be destroyed."[7] Quite right. But Cunningham does not go on to draw the natural conclusion to these remarks; that precisely because they attain such unity (though remaining distinct), the lovers perish in a mutual flame. They *do* remain distinct; but that paradoxical relationship, as Cunningham shows, is conceived of in terms of the mystical relations of the Trinity. And this suggests that such a relationship is possible only in the supra-human order.

This, I think, is what misleads Cunningham in his interpretation of the threnos. He sees the death of the lovers as a triumphant transcendence of mortality, and he invokes a Platonic eschatology, which is only partially warranted by the poem: "The lovers are of course destroyed in that they have passed in a mutual flame from this life, but clearly they have only passed into the real life of Ideas from the unreal life of materiality." [8] But the emphatic note of the threnos, as I have suggested, is not the immortality (either here or there) of the Phoenix (and her beloved), but their complete extinction. *Human* love will not admit of the complete oneness of the lovers. Such unity leads, for human beings, to death. And that is why the threnos focuses so emphatically on the lovers' complete extinction. The kind of love described in the anthem leads to the mutual flame in which the lovers perish (in the threnos).

This (implicit) connection between anthem and threnos is slightly supported by the wry *double entendre* involved in their "dying," which is itself supported by the secondary, sexual meaning of stanza 16:

> Leaving no posterity:
> 'Twas not their infirmity,
> It was married chastity.

These lines have been taken as somewhat ludicrous, "almost like a Falstaffian quip at some over fanatic Puritan pair."[9] But though there is an undertone of wry humor produced by the sexual meaning, the chief meaning of these lines (certified by the lines that follow) is that (1) the Phoenix does not give birth at its death to a new Phoenix, and (2) Truth and Beauty and perfect Love (the Ideas) perish with the Phoenix and Turtle in whom they are embodied.

It is in these two senses that the lovers leave no posterity. In stanza 6, what seems at first glance a hyperbolic compliment—the identification of Love and Constancy (the Ideas) with the Phoenix and the Turtle—

turns out to be quite literally meant.[10] When the Phoenix and the Turtle perish, they take away with them all particular truth and beauty—which depend for their existence on these Ideal Forms. That is why Reason now laments that

> Truth may seem, but cannot be;
> Beauty brag, but 'tis not she:
> Truth and Beauty buried be.

The true and fair who are urged at the end to sigh a prayer for these dead birds are those who only *seem* true and fair. For the Phoenix and Turtle have left, alas, no posterity.

This conclusion is related in yet another way to the anthem. The perfection of their love, their being neither one nor two, but rather both one and two—this means that they cannot be anything *but* chaste, for concupiscence in such a relationship is not possible. "Either was the other's mine." Their lack of posterity is therefore not a result of "infirmity," but of married chastity in this sense. Paradoxically and ironically, this chastity is figured in a consummation, a mutual flame (analogous to the erotic one), which leads to annihilation.

If this analysis of the poem is accurate, then the poem does not, as A. Alvarez has urged, presage the triumphant vision of human love—the quasi-mystical humanism—of Shakespeare's late plays.[11] This sort of interpretation rests chiefly on the assumption that the Phoenix is, in some sense and in accordance with tradition, reborn. But Shakespeare's Phoenix dies and is gone forever. It is gone forever from this world, at any rate—which is the only world our poem is concerned with.

It is rather with the dramatic work of 1600-04 that the poem ought to be associated, with *Hamlet, Troilus,* and *Othello. Hamlet* is not thematically focused on love, but we may discern in the idealism and skepticism of Hamlet himself something of the mood of our poem. It is present in Hamlet's revulsion at his mother's unchastity and in his skepticism about the possibility of goodness in man, that paragon of animals and quintessence of dust. *Troilus and Cressida* is even more bitter. In the world of the play neither love nor honor can exist—not, at any rate, the real thing. Truth may seem, but it cannot be. Troilus may delude himself, but we know his passion for what it is—and so does Cressida. Helen is not worth what she doth cost the keeping. The Greeks are driven by passion and appetite. Achilles himself turns out to be a cowardly cutthroat. All the argument is a whore and a cuckold. In *Othello* we get a profound vision of the inevitable imperfection in human love, and its apparent causelessness. For Othello is a good man, and Desdemona is an ideal woman. But Love and Constancy are dead.

Ellrodt comes close to the position I would take with respect to the poem's relation to Shakespeare's other work:

The very mood of the poem . . . would admirably suit the state of mind one may reasonably ascribe to Shakespeare in 1600-1. . . . The union of Truth and Beauty achieved in the mutual flame of the Phoenix and the Turtle is contrasted with their present divorce in a world which may still hold lovers "either true or fair," but cannot allow "the pure union of the two qualities in one and the same woman." In such a mood did Hamlet send Ophelia to a nunnery. In a mood hardly different did the dramatist in his later plays lodge "beauty, truth and rarity" in *one* woman, *one* Phoenix-creature, miraculously preserved from this world's taints, like Marina among the bawds, Perdita among her flowers, Miranda on her desert island.[12]

I disagree only with Ellrodt's last sentence. The late romances seem to me to contain an intuition that human love is, for all its imperfection, possible —is, indeed, a miraculous source of joy and immortality. That is the vision expressed preeminently in *Antony and Cleopatra*, where the very imperfection of humanity makes possible self-transcendence. Human love is not platonized; it is rooted in the senses and in mortal human bodies. By fully accepting their mortal status, Antony and Cleopatra attain a kind of immortality. This is a radically different view of human possibilities from the one we find in "The Phoenix and Turtle."

NOTES

CHAPTER ONE

1. According to my reckoning the following sonnets are in the three groups: the "breed" group includes 1-14, 16-17; the eternizing group includes 15, 18, 19, 54, 55, 60, 63, 65, 81, 100, 101, 107; the constancy group includes 25, 116, 123, 124, 125. Of the 126 sonnets of the Fair Youth series, 41 deal explicitly with Time the Destroyer. In addition to the sonnets already listed, these include those sonnets which simply lament the triumph of Time over the beloved (64, 77, 104, 126) or over the poet (71-74).

2. These ideas are explicit in 78, 79, and 100. In 79 the beloved's being constitutes the rival poet's invention. In 78 the beloved is "all my art." The rival poet, though he is admitted to be a better poet, does *not* confer immortality on the beloved—which suggests that it is love, rather than artistry, which "causes" immortality.

On the beloved's living in verse, see 17, 19, 55, 63, 65, 74.

3. Yvor Winters, *Forms of Discovery* (n.p., 1967), p. 57.

4. G. W. Knight (*The Mutual Flame* [London, 1955], p. 87) remarks that the poetry "is shown as not merely a perpetuating instrument, but a way of making contact with, or mentally entering, or possessing the wondrous thing. There is a reciprocity between the object and the poetry, and it may be hard to say which is the most indebted to the other." Knight also says (p. 86) that the poet

is aware of some miraculous possibility. The truth is, that there is indeed a poetic "miracle," but it is not just a matter of publication and perpetuity. Rather the poet knows that through his poetry, or the poetic consciousness, he establishes, or focusses, a supernal reality, or truth, what we may call a "poetic dimension," that cannot otherwise be attained; and of this the written poetry ("black ink"), though it be necessary, is really subsidiary.

5. I am indebted to my student Mrs. Joan Hellman for pointing out to me the importance of the distilling sonnets.

6. In 74 the poet says that his soul will survive, after his body's death, in "this" (the poem).

7. The first crux is in line 8: since "calls" is transitive, either "time" or "fashion" must be its subject and the alternate word its object. "Time" makes sense as subject, but "fashion" makes almost none as object. Construed the other way, the whole clause makes no sense. I think an emendation is needed. I would read "passion" for "fashion." This gives an intelligible object for "calls" and is orthographically plausible.

The second crux is the last line: In what sense do the "fools of time" "die for goodness"? Ingram and Redpath (*Shakespeare's Sonnets* [London, 1964], pp. 284-85) interpret the phrase thus: "after a life of wrong-doing, [they] renounce their time serving . . . to die for permanent values." But this seems much too explicit. I would suggest that the fools of time *illustrate by their death* the superiority of the opposite way of life. T. G. Tucker (*The Sonnets of Shakespeare* [Cambridge, 1924], p. 204) remarks: "These persons may be 'called to witness' as having learned by experience —or as conspicuous examples of the fact—that 'policy' which 'works on short leases' is not the best policy. . . ." Cf. 125, where the poet calls upon time servers to bear witness to the waste of their lives.

CHAPTER TWO

1. On Shakespeare's ambivalence in the histories, see A. P. Rossiter's brilliant essay "Ambivalence: The Dialectic of the Histories," in *Angel with Horns* (New York, 1961), pp. 40-64.

2. E. K. Chambers remarks (*William Shakespeare* [Oxford, 1930], 1.399) that one feature of the play is "an extreme simplicity both of vocabulary and of phrasing" which sometimes leads "to a stiffness, perhaps even a baldness, of diction," reminiscent of pre-Shakespearean plays.

3. Shakespeare's changes in Plutarch's Caesar are incisively dealt with by M. W. MacCallum (*Shakespeare's Roman Plays and Their Background* [London, 1910], p. 226). See Also Virgil Whitaker, *Shakespeare's Use of Learning* (San Marino, Calif., 1953), pp. 230-34.

4. See the discussion of the traditional ambivalence toward Caesar, which was inherited by the Elizabethans, by Geoffrey Bullough, *Narrative and Dramatic Sources of Shakespeare* (New York, 1964), 5.1-24.

5. See *Hamlet* III.iii.11-23.

6. I cannot agree with G. W. Knight's observation (*The Imperial Theme* [London, 1951], pp. 63-64) that the play "has, as it were, four protagonists, each with a different view of the action." Knight does not explain this remark.

7. Ibid., p. 63.

8. Plutarch does not refer to any affection of Brutus for Caesar.

9. Brents Sterling (*Unity in Shakespearian Tragedy* [New York, 1956], pp. 40-54) analyzes the whole play from this point of view.

10. In Plutarch the populace is moved to anger at the conspirators by Brutus' speech.

11. An additional ironic view of the upshot of the conspiracy is given in IV.i, where Antony, Octavius, and Lepidus "prick" those who are to die as though they were killing flies. One of the proscribed is Lepidus' brother, to whose death Lepidus casually consents. Another is Antony's sister's son; "Look, with a spot I damn him," says Antony. The thematic relevance of the scene is obvious.

12. Whitaker, pp. 244-45.

13. Ibid., pp. 235-36.

14. In Plutarch the quarrel and the appearance of the ghost are widely separated incidents.

CHAPTER THREE

1. See the *New Variorum Edition,* ed. Hillebrand and Baldwin (Philadelphia, 1953), pp. 519-70.

2. E. M. W. Tillyard (*Shakespeare's Problem Plays* [London, 1950], pp. 33-88 *passim*) refers to the play's stylistic "inflation and deflation." T. McAlindon ("Language, Style, and Meaning in *Troilus and Cressida,*" *PMLA* 84 [Jan. 1969]: 29-43) describes the play's violations of stylistic decorum. He sees these discords as expressing the violation by all the chief characters of a moral code implicit in the play. This seems to me a mistaken, though pious, inference. My own view, as will appear, is that the tonal equivocation, in conjunction with other structural features, points to the nonexistence and the impossibility of any such code.

3. As W. W. Lawrence would see him here. See his article "Troilus, Cressida and Thersites," *MLR* 36 (1942): 430.

4. Alice Walker recognizes the subtle mockery directed at Troilus and the Greek commanders, but accepts the prologue as "dignified." See her introduction to the Cambridge edition (1957), p. xvii.

5. Nevill Coghill is the only critic I know who sees this clearly. See his *Shakespeare's Professional Skills* (Cambridge, 1964), p. 111.

6. Tillyard (p. 46) says that Troilus here expresses a "noble devotion."

7. The terms are O. J. Campbell's. See his *Comicall Satyre and Shakespeare's* Troilus and Cressida (San Marino, Calif. 1959), pp. 211-12.

8. Cf. Robert Ornstein, *The Moral Vision of Jacobean Tragedy* (Madison, 1960), p. 241.

9. I differ here slightly but significantly from Coghill, who writes (p. 118): "It is this power in woman to elicit in man the things that he esteems as his glories which is at the core of courtly love. . . . For Troilus, it is Cressida who has this power: her beauty in rousing sensual desire rouses idealism, till he can almost believe that she too is touched with it. . . ."

10. Cf. David Kaula, "Will and Reason in *Troilus and Cressida,*" *SQ* 12 (1961): 272: "If Troilus is basically a sensualist, then his constant preoccupation with truth, honor, simplicity, and so forth seems very much beside the point. If he is an inspired idealist, then surely not much value can be attached to an idealism so egregiously incapable of coming to terms with the existent world. The real Troilus seems to lie somewhere between the two extremes."

11. Tillyard (p. 65) remarks that while Troilus is "defective in wit but

strong in will," Hector is "just the opposite."

12. Coghill, pp. 120-121.

13. Tillyard (p. 63) finds the change in Troilus from a "mercurial lover to the fiercely resolute and overmastering young commander . . . too violent to be swallowed without effort." But the "change" is clear and credible.

14. See also II.i.50f., II.iii.78f., III.iii.312f., V.i.53f., V.i.96f., V.ii.55f., V.ii.193f.

15. Kittredge, ed., *Complete Works of Shakespeare* (1936), p. 880.

16. Tillyard, p. 60.

17. The same sort of corrupt eroticism is expressed in Pandarus' song at III.i.125-36, and indeed in this whole scene.

18. Tillyard, p. 85.

19. Coghill, p. 127.

20. Cf. Kaula, p. 283.

CHAPTER FOUR

1. "The *Othello* Music," in *The Wheel of Fire*, 4th ed. (London, 1954), p. 109.

2. See Inga-Stina Ekeblad, "The 'Impure Art' of John Webster," *RES* 9 (August, 1958): 253-67; and T. S. Eliot, *Selected Essays* (New York, 1950), pp. 96-97.

3. *The Wheel of Fire*, pp. 101-6.

4. I refer to *Troilus and Cressida* III.ii.20-26:

> Th' imaginary relish is so sweet
> That it enchants my sense. What will it be
> When that the watery palates taste indeed
> Love's thrice-repured nectar? Death, I fear me;
> Sounding destruction; or some joy too fine,
> Too subtle-potent, tuned too sharp in sweetness
> For the capacity of my ruder powers.

5. *The Wheel of Fire*, p. 11.

6. See F. R. Leavis, "Diabolic Intellect and the Noble Hero," in *The Common Pursuit* (London, 1962), pp. 136-59.

CHAPTER FIVE

1. John D. Rosenberg, "King Lear and His Comforters," *Essays in Criticism* 16 (1966): 136-46. See also Barbara Everett, "The New King Lear," *Critical Quarterly* 2 (1960): 325-39.

2. Rosenberg, p. 137.

3. Ibid., p. 146.

4. A. C. Bradley, *Shakespearean Tragedy*, Meridian Books (Cleveland and New York, 1955), pp. 258-59.

5. Freud, *Collected Papers*, IV (London, 1950, p. 255.

6. Ibid., p. 253.

7. Ibid.

8. Ibid., p. 256.

9. John F. Danby, *Shakespeare's Doctrine of Nature* (London, 1948).
10. Ibid., p. 35.
11. William R. Elton, "King Lear" *and the Gods* (San Marino, 1966), pp. 145-70.
12. Danby, p. 113.
13. Ibid.
14. G. W. Knight, *The Wheel of Fire*, p. 168.
15. Gloucester's mimed fall off the Dover cliff parallels Lear's confrontation of nothingness. See Jan Kott's remarkable analysis of this scene, showing how the scene's "absurd" theatricality precisely expresses the nonliteralness of Gloucester's leap, that is to say, its metaphysical meaning: in *"King Lear*, or Endgame,"* in *Shakespeare, Our Contemporary*, Anchor Books (New York, 1966), pp. 142-51.
16. Maynard Mack, *King Lear in Our Time* (Berkeley, 1965) p. 117.

One of the most puzzling sentiments in this pagan and brutal play is the recurrent notion that men must endure their going hence. One would suppose that in the light of the world's cruelty and godlessness, suicide would be a quite reasonable act. Why must they have patience, why is ripeness all? I have no answer. I would note, however, that all the good characters in the play, in the face of misery and pain maintain their dignity *by giving themselves to others, by acts of love*. Perhaps "enduring" is a form of this love, a sacrifice which makes no sense in worldly terms.

CHAPTER SEVEN

1. G. Wilson Knight (*The Imperial Theme* [London, 1951], p. xi) discerns the cause of the reductive tendency in academic criticism. There is, he says,

in the human mind a strong reluctance to face, with full consciousness, the products of poetic genius; and this often takes the form of an attempt to reduce them to something *other*, to read them either in terms of some lesser attribute within themselves more readily assimilable to an intellectual inquiry, or in terms of their age; that is, of modern histories and of forgotten, and comparatively non-significant works. This, our natural academic tendency, is of appalling, and insidious strength. Whereas a vital interpretation trying to do justice to Shakespearian poetry in its wholeness and its power must always be suspect, approval awaits anyone who more safely reduces it to characterization, or stage-technique, or statistics of imagery, applying to such parts, or aspects, a scholarly precision that *looks* very effective, but which has nevertheless, by concentrating on a part and forgetting the whole, quite failed to do justice to the essential life and amplitude of the work concerned.

2. W. K. Wimsatt, Jr., "The Structure of the 'Concrete Universal' in Literature," in *Criticism: The Foundations of Modern Literary Judgment*, ed. Schorer, Miles, and McKenzie (New York, 1958), p. 402.
3. Ethel Seaton, in *"Antony and Cleopatra* and the *Book of Revelation,"* *RES* 22 (July, 1946): 219-24, points out that much of the play's extraordinary imagery is derived from the *Book of Revelation*. She observes (p. 224) that one effect of this imagery is to "enforce the conviction that this most worldly pair, children of luxury and riot, must indeed be viewed

sub specie aeternitatis, as if children of light." The full implications of Miss Seaton's discovery will emerge in the course of our analysis.

4. Throughout this chapter I am assuming a theory of human love which is presented eloquently in M. C. D'Arcy's *The Mind and Heart of Love* (New York, 1947). D'Arcy distinguishes two kinds of human love—in everyday terms, the selfish and unselfish—related to the two basic tendencies in human personality, Animus and Anima. The Animus includes all those drives toward self-betterment and possession which are connected with the rational in man. The Anima includes those tendencies toward self-giving which are related to the emotional side of personality, everything which is either below or beyond reason. It treats the other as another "I" rather than as a thing to be possessed. Though these tendencies are called masculine and feminine, the full development of human personality in man or woman requires the proper development of each.

The pattern of change which I describe in Antony, and which is crucial for an understanding of the play, involves a shift from an overdominance of Animus to a recognition of the claims of Anima. He begins by regarding Cleopatra as a thing, an object to be exploited; he ends by recognizing her as a person, thereby becoming fully a person himself. I have hesitated to use D'Arcy's terminology for fear of imposing alien categories on the play. Though D'Arcy's theory illuminates the play, it is not, after all, Shakespeare's. Shakespeare is more humanistic than D'Arcy: he roots the value of human love in purely natural experience rather than in God.

5. It is a mark of Bradley's acuity that, unlike many of his disciples, he recognizes both the play's greatness and its radical difference from the other tragedies. He observes (*Oxford Lectures on Poetry* [London, 1909], p. 292) that "the positive element in the final impression, the element of reconciliation, is strongly emphasised. The peculiar effect of the drama depends partly, as we have seen, on the absence of decidedly tragic scenes and events in its first half; but it depends quite as much on this emphasis." Later (p. 305) he remarks that the play "attempts something different, and succeeds as triumphantly as *Othello* itself. In doing so it gives us what no other tragedy can give. . . ."

6. *The Imperial Theme*, pp. 22-23. On the "morality" of literature, see also Robert Ornstein, "Historical Criticism and the Interpretation of Shakespeare," *SQ* 10 (winter, 1959):3-9. Ornstein remarks (*The Moral Vision of Jacobean Tragedy* [Madison, 1960], p. 4) that "the moral apprehension of drama is an aesthetic experience which depends upon the immediately created impression of character, thought, and action."

CHAPTER EIGHT

1. S. L. Bethell, *The Winter's Tale: A Study* (London, n. d.).

2. G. Wilson Knight, *The Crown of Life* (London, 1947), pp. 76-127.

3. Note that in this passage Florizel imputes a kind of *natural* divinity to Perdita. He sees her as a "presence" in the very processes of Nature, and he rejoices in it. He also connects her with the eternal.

4. Edward W. Tayler, *Nature and Art in Renaissance Literature* (New

York, 1964). See also Frank Kermode's introduction to the Arden *Tempest*.

5. Arthur C. Kirsch, "*Cymbeline* and Coterie Dramaturgy," in *Shakespeare's Later Comedies*, ed. D. J. Palmer, Penguin Books (Harmondsworth, 1971), pp. 264-90. This essay first appeared in *ELH* 34 (1967): 285-306.

6. Kirsch (p. 282) makes the acute remark that "There is no need, in this case as with any other, to assume that the interior logic of Shakespeare's artistic development is at odds with his theatrical environment."

APPENDIX B

1. Robert Ellrodt, "An Anatomy of 'The Phoenix and the Turtle,'" *Shakespeare Survey* 15 (1962): 99-110; Murray Copland, "The Dead Phoenix," *Essays in Criticism* 15 (July, 1965): 279-87.

2. See G. Wilson Knight, *The Mutual Flame* (London, 1962), pp. 203-4; T. W. Baldwin, *On the Literary Genetics of Shakespeare's Poems and Sonnets* (Urbana, 1950), pp. 363-64, 368; I. A. Richards, "The Sense of Poetry: Shakespeare's 'The Phoenix and the Turtle,'" in *Symbolism in Religion and Literature*, ed. Rollo May (New York, 1961), pp. 203-14. Knight (p. 203) adduces a passage from Lactantius' *Carmen de Phoenice;* but the passage says only that the Phoenix's voice is "sweeter than any earthly strain." F. T. Prince, the editor of the 1960 Arden edition of the Poems, remarks (p. 179 n.) that "most commentators agree that this bird's identity is left uncertain. . . . The meaning is probably that whatever bird proves able to sing loudest should act as a herald."

3. Ellrodt says (p. 108) that "any hint of survival in a world beyond is withheld."

4. Ronald Bates, "Shakespeare's 'The Phoenix and the Turtle,'" *Shakespeare Quarterly* 6 (winter, 1955): 19-30.

5. See L. Charbonneau-Lassay, *Le Bestiaire du Christ* (Desclée, 1940), p. 634. That this tradition survives to Shakespeare's time is indicated in *Hamlet* I.i.149-64. Note that the swan's role is also functional in terms of its legendary powers.

6. J. V. Cunningham, "Idea as Structure: *The Phoenix and the Turtle*," in *Tradition and Poetic Structure* (Denver, 1960), pp. 76-89.

7. Ibid. p. 85.

8. Ibid. See also S. M. Bonaventure, "The Phoenix Renewed," *Ball State Teachers College Forum* 5 (autumn, 1964): 76.

9. Bates, p. 28.

10. For a similar hyperbolic praise, which remains figurative, cf. Ben Jonson's "Though Beautie be the Marke of praise," from which I quote three stanzas:

> His falling Temples [Love's] you have rear'd
> The withered Garlands tane away;
> His Altars kept from the Decay,
> That envie wish'd, and Nature fear'd.
>
> And on them, burne so chaste a flame,
> With so much Loyalties expence
> As Love t'aquit such excellence
> Is gone himselfe into your Nam~

> And you are he: the Deitie
> To whom all Lovers are design'd;
> That would their better objects find:
> Among which faithfull troope am I.

11. A. Alvarez, "The Phoenix and the Turtle," in *Interpretations,* ed. John Wain (London, 1955), p. 16. See also G. W. Knight, *The Mutual Flame* (London, 1955), p. 204; *The Imperial Theme* (London, 1951), pp. 349-50; and Daniel Seltzer, "Their Tragic Scene: *The Phoenix and the Turtle,*" *Shakespeare Quarterly* 12 (spring, 1961): 102.
12. Ellrodt, p. 108.

INDEX

Elias Schwartz, who holds advanced degrees from New York University, the University of Chicago, and Stanford, is Professor of English at the State University of New York at Binghamton. He is the author of *The Forms of Feeling* (Kennikat, 1972) and has published numerous articles on Shakespeare, Chapman, and literary theory.